More Praise for *The Flag, the Poet & the Song*

"You'll sound very smart after you read this charming, trivia-filled book."
— *The Arizona Republic*

"Irvin Molotsky's welcome revisionist book clarifies, corrects, or finds irony in a number of points in early American history that we take for granted."
— *Albuquerque Journal*

"An informative and iconoclastic journey through the writing of 'The Star-Spangled Banner' and the assorted barnacles of history that since then have clung to the national anthem."
— *The Hartford Courant*

"A lively wrapping up of the life story of Francis Scott Key and an account of the growing popularity of the poem that became the national anthem."
— *The Orlando Sentinel*

"A well-researched account of how the flag and the song came forever to be linked in one of those fateful moments where if one element had failed, all would fail."
— *Richmond Times-Dispatch*

IRVIN MOLOTSKY is a reporter and editor with the Washington bureau of *The New York Times*. He lives with his wife, Iris, in Washington, D.C.

Also by Irvin Molotsky

The Great Mail Order Bazaar (1986)

The Flag, the Poet and the Song

THE STORY OF THE STAR-SPANGLED BANNER

Irvin Molotsky

A PLUME BOOK

PLUME
Published by the Penguin Group
Penguin Putnam Inc., 375 Hudson Street, New York, New York 10014, U.S.A.
Penguin Books Ltd, 27 Wrights Lane, London W8 5TZ, England
Penguin Books Australia Ltd, Ringwood, Victoria, Australia
Penguin Books Canada Ltd, 10 Alcorn Avenue, Toronto,
Ontario, Canada M4V 3B2
Penguin Books (N.Z.) Ltd, 182–190 Wairau Road, Auckland 10, New Zealand

Penguin Books Ltd, Registered Offices: Harmondsworth, Middlesex, England

Published by Plume, a member of Penguin Putnam Inc.
Previously published in a Dutton edition.

First Plume Printing, December 2001
1   3   5   7   9   10   8   6   4   2

Ⓟ REGISTERED TRADEMARK — MARCA REGISTRADA

The Library of Congress has catalogued the Dutton edition as follows:
Molotsky, Irvin.
The flag, the poet & the song : the story of the
Star-Spangled Banner / Irvin Molotsky.
p.   cm.
ISBN 0-525-94600-4 (hc.)
ISBN 0-452-28345-0 (pbk.)
1. Baltimore, Battle of, 1814. 2. United States—History—War of 1812—Flags.
3. Flags—United States—History—19th century. 4. Star-spangled banner (Song)
5. Key, Francis Scott, 1779–1843. 6. United States—History—War of 1812—
Influence. I. Title: Flag, the poet, and the song. II. Title.

E356.B2 M65 2001
973.5'2—dc21
2001017325

Printed in the United States of America
Original hardcover design by Leonard Telesca

To Iris, as Always

Contents

Photo/Illustration Credits

Page 104–105: National Park Service, Fort McHenry, NMHS

Page 110: The Conway Library, Courtauld Institute of Art

Page 118: Maryland Historical Society

Page 119: National Park Service: Fort McHenry, NMHS

Page 121: Lossing, *Field Manual of the War of 1812*

Page 135: Angel Art Ltd.

Page 140: National Museum of American History, Smithsonian Institution

Page 143: National Museum of American History, Smithsonian Institution

Page 178: AP/WIDE WORLD PHOTO/Joe Rosenthal

Page 180: AP/WIDE WORLD PHOTO/Charles Tasnadi

Page 214: Thomas Franklin, *The Bergen Record*, Corbis SABA

Introduction

Sometimes it seems that the last two words of "The Star-Spangled Banner" are "play ball!" Our national anthem has become so identified with sports events that it has, in many ways, become trivialized. We sing it by rote, without thought, or we listen to it, but we do not hear the words. Repetition has robbed it of much of its meaning. Much the same can be said for the flag that "The Star-Spangled Banner" celebrates. In many places, those "broad stripes and bright stars" become little more than a prop for a used-car lot at a Washington's Birthday sale or a political candidate trying to show the voters that he is more patriotic than his opponent.

It was not always so. The song that was to become our national anthem was written in 1814, but the earliest account of the first performance of "The Star-Spangled Banner" at a baseball game has put it at 1862, and that account is dubious. It is more likely that baseball's first use of the national anthem did not come until the twentieth century. This is just one of the myths and facts that must be sifted through in the telling of the story of the Star-Spangled Banner—actually a three-part story, since it takes in the flag, which led to the poem, which led to the song that became our national anthem. The flag is, of course, the Stars and Stripes, Old Glory, and it has the power to inspire us. It also has so much symbolic power that people protesting or advocating one thing or another are led to parade under it or even to set it on fire.

Before we get to the story, some background is necessary. Much of that background concerns the War of 1812, a conflict that most Americans know nothing about. What kind of a war is named after a year? In the days leading up to the War of 1812, Francis Scott Key is a lawyer and poet who is little known outside of Washington and Maryland. His sudden moment of everlasting inspiration, the composition of "The Star-Spangled Banner," is yet to come. Also not well known, even to this day, are three other people who will play major roles in this story—Mary Pickersgill, who made the flag that inspired Key; Major George Armistead, whose defense of Fort McHenry saved Baltimore and who flew Pickersgill's flag; and Major General Robert Ross, a gallant British soldier whose death in battle may have assured the American victory at Fort McHenry.

The War of 1812 had real military and political consequences, and it also planted the seeds that led eventually
to the veneration of the flag, something that is not found
widely outside America. After almost two centuries, that
original Fort McHenry Star-Spangled Banner still exists,
though it does not still wave. It is in the tender, loving care
of the Smithsonian Institution in Washington and is probably good for at least another two hundred years—maybe a
thousand years more, if conservators are correct. Americans still struggle through the singing of our national anthem and the words of Key's poem, which speaks of the
flag waving over the land of the free—a poem written by a
man who owned slaves. Key was a poet, a patriot and, yes,
a slaveholder. That is not the only irony in our tale. The
flag so honored by Americans from the war between the
United States and Britain was sewn together of cloth that
was probably made in Britain. And Key set his words to
the music of an old English drinking song. We sing it
today, although it is beyond the range of most untrained
voices. This is the story of that flag, and of that poem and
that song, and the man who wrote them.

A few notes on style. Two terms that occur throughout
this book—describing a flag and a song—have the same
name, so here is the practice that I have adopted to avoid
confusion. "The Star-Spangled Banner" (within quotes and
The capitalized) is the song and the poem, but the Star-
Spangled Banner is the flag.

In a second attempt to avoid confusion—or at least

distraction — I have adopted standardized American modern spelling, even in direct quotations from letters and official reports. This has the effect of slightly changing some spellings but not changing any meanings at all. During much of the time that this book covers, the early nineteenth century, spelling was not yet standardized. Some people, for example, spelled that big bay as Chesapeake, as we do today, but others spelled it without the "e" on the end. It is not a matter of one being right and the other wrong, because both were correct and in wide use at the time, but one spelling eventually prevailed.

The Flag, the Poet and the Song

1

The Star-Spangled Baritone and the Clocker

Today "The Star-Spangled Banner" is played before every baseball, football, basketball, hockey and soccer game in the United States, and fans in the stands dutifully and patriotically rise and sing, but the television networks are cleverer. They sell that time to sponsors for their beer and car and razor commercials. The players have to stand at attention and have to remember not to scratch themselves in an embarrassing place lest it be noticed. Only in Baltimore and Atlanta, so far as I know, do baseball fans really pay attention to the national anthem, in both cases because they have modified it as a sort of rally song. To understand what happens in Baltimore, it must be known that the team, the Orioles, are known as the O's, which is no doubt a newspaper invention to allow the name to be squeezed into a narrow headline. When I was a boy, my hometown Philadelphia Athletics were known as the A's, a nickname that followed them to Kansas City and Oakland.

The song is begun normally and proceeds normally, but when the second-to-last line is reached, "O say, does that star-spangled banner yet wave," the *O* is shouted by everyone in the park. Get it? Very funny in Baltimore. Scared the hell out of me the first time I heard it. Think of the effect of forty thousand or so people waiting quietly and politely during almost all of the national anthem and then shouting, "O!" Now I shout it too. In Atlanta, the fans fight off boredom during the anthem by modifying the last line to "O'er the land of the free and the home of the Braves." Get it? The Braves! Very funny in Atlanta.

"The Star-Spangled Banner" turns up at the oddest places. Many opera companies open their seasons with it, and whenever I am at opening night at the Washington Opera the audience includes some people with trained voices—frustrated opera singers, no doubt—and they are just about the only ones who can manage the anthem's wide range. The soprano Licia Albanese attended opening nights at the Metropolitan Opera in New York City for twenty-five years so that she could join in the singing of the national anthem from her seat in the grand tier box. At least the opera houses don't begin every performance with it, just opening night. It is also sung before heavyweight boxing championships, or at least it was before I stopped watching them. Sometimes the anthem lasted longer than the bout.

How did we get to this point where "The Star-Spangled Banner" has been sung so often that it has lost its impact? We probably have baseball to blame for that, but the origins remain uncertain despite years of research. The Baseball Hall of Fame in Cooperstown, New York, cites *The Cultural Encyclopedia of Baseball* by Jonathan Fraser Light, which says: "Although the National Baseball Library cannot document the first time the anthem was played at a baseball game, it is believed that the song was played on May 15, 1862, during the Civil War at the opening of the Capitoline Grounds," which were in the Bedford-Stuyvesant section of Brooklyn. This is dubious, and so is the encyclopedia's suggestion that one of the earliest performances in the twentieth century was for a game played by the New York Highlanders, now the Yankees, on April 30, 1903. Recording and public address systems had not yet been developed enough to allow recorded performances, so the performances would have had to have been by brass bands, an expensive proposition, and they usually would be reserved for special occasions. In any event, there is not good documentation to these earlier performances. The first well-documented performance of "The Star-Spangled Banner" at a baseball game came at Comiskey Park during the 1918 World Series between the Chicago Cubs and the Boston Red Sox, a time of heightened patriotism because of American participation in World War I. The Cubs, a National League team, played in

Comiskey Park, the home of the White Sox in the American League? Yes, in baseball's never-ending quest for more revenue, the leagues forced the Cubs to play their home games in the larger park of their South Side rivals. During the opening game, a 1–0 pitchers' duel won by Babe Ruth for Boston, a Navy band struck up "The Star-Spangled Banner" during the seventh-inning stretch, and the crowd joined in singing.

Because of wartime travel restrictions, the 1918 World Series was played in a three-four format—three games at the first team's park and four games at the second—instead of the two-three-two schedule used today. When the series shifted to Boston, with the Red Sox enjoying a two-to-one advantage, the Red Sox owner, Harry Frazee, also had the national anthem performed, but he put it on before the game started. This led to the practice of having "The Star-Spangled Banner" performed before each season's opening day and at the beginning of World Series games, so Frazee perhaps had made his first dubious music-related decision.

His second one was worse, at least for Boston. In 1920, in order to help finance a Broadway musical that he was producing, *No, No, Nanette,* Frazee sold baseball's greatest player, Babe Ruth, to the New York Yankees for $125,000 and a $300,000 loan. Older references to money are not very useful if current-day equivalents are not given, and the sale price of $125,000 is the equivalent of $1,068,000 today, according to tables compiled by Professor Robert C. Sahr of Oregon State University. The $300,000 loan is worth $2,564,000 today. I would say the Yankees got quite a bargain. *No, No, Nanette* finally made it to Broadway in 1925 and contained two of the best songs written in that era, "Tea for Two" and "I Want to Be Happy," music by Vincent Youmans and lyrics by Irving Caesar and Otto Harbach. Both Yankee fans and Broadway musical fans should say, "Thank you, Harry Frazee."

David Marasco, a baseball historian, delights in this assessment by *The New York Times* at the conclusion of the 1918 World Series, which the Red Sox won: "The 1918 triumph marks the fifth World Series that the Red Sox have brought to the highbrow domicile of the baked bean. Boston is the luckiest baseball spot on earth, for it has never lost a World Series." Boston's luck ran out. The Red Sox have lost every World Series they've appeared in since that dreadful sale of Babe Ruth to the Yankees, and some say they will never win because of the Curse of the Bambino. Maybe the Red Sox could exorcise the curse and win their first Series since 1918 by ending the practice of playing the national anthem before every game. It's worth trying.

As it had during World War I, wartime patriotism led to the national anthem being played before every major league baseball game in World War II, starting with the 1942 season. Not everyone welcomed this repetition. In time—according to *The Cultural Encyclopedia of Baseball*—a sportswriter named Ken Smith, later director of the Baseball Hall of Fame, said, "For Christ's sake, we're running a business here. Does Macy's play 'The Star-Spangled

Banner' before opening its doors every day?" Nicely put, Mr. Smith.

I could do very nicely without "The Star-Spangled Banner" before every sporting event. So could Robert Goulet. He is a very good singer, but if you mention his name, most people, if they are old enough, will first remember the time he messed up the national anthem before the 1965 heavyweight championship boxing match between Muhammad Ali and Sonny Liston. This is how David Remnick describes what happened in his excellent biography of Ali, *King of the World*:

> The honor of singing the national anthem went to Robert Goulet, a slick heartthrob singer made for Las Vegas and fight nights. But this would not be his finest night in the ring. As Goulet walked from his dressing room, he fumbled around in his pockets and discovered that he had lost his "palm notes," the lyrics to "The Star-Spangled Banner."
>
> "What am I going to do?" Goulet murmured to himself as he stepped through the ropes and into the ring. Then it turned out that he could barely hear the organ music accompanying him. He flubbed the lyrics and had a hard time keeping pace with the tune; it was as if he were a small child struggling to keep pace with a parent in a rush.

Because of his name, pronounced goo-LAY, I had always assumed that he was from Canada and was willing to excuse the flub. But it turned out that he was born in Lawrence, Massachusetts, to French-Canadian parents, and he had plenty of time to hear it over and over before he moved with his family to Canada when he was thirteen years old.

There were other sporting events with unfortunate renditions of the national anthem, which television does carry for championship games like the World Series. In 1969, Jose Feliciano offended many people with his very slow folk-rock, highly stylized version before a World Series game in Detroit between the Tigers and the St. Louis Cardinals. It is not well known, but Feliciano was a last-minute replacement for the country singer Eddie Arnold, who would not have offended anyone but decided against performing, concluding that he couldn't do it justice, thereby winning the candor award. Feliciano was cheered by some people in the stadium but booed by more. Jim Campbell, then president of the Detroit Tigers, told *The New York Times*, "We were so busy that we never auditioned Jose. As soon as he started singing, a real personalized, hip version of the anthem, our switchboard lit up and telegrams began pouring in from people who were complaining. Of course, there were some people who liked it, but I and the Tigers really took a lot of heat over the incident and so did the baseball commissioner's office." On the positive side, Campbell said, "I think we made Jose famous. He admits that now in television talk shows and in interviews. I think he is a wonderful artist, but he'll never sing that rendition of the national anthem again in any ball park I run." Feliciano was the first singer to offer a nontraditional version of the national anthem at a major sports event, and the reaction hurt his career for a time, but he came back after the complaints died down.

The Feliciano flap was nothing compared to the outcry that followed the performance before a San Diego Padres game on July 25, 1990, by the television comedienne Roseanne Barr, who was, well, gross. Her performance was intentionally terrible and she ended by grabbing her crotch and spitting in parody of baseball players. The Broadway singer Patti LuPone is one star who did well when called upon to perform for country and sports. She sang "The Star-Spangled Banner" at a sports event for the first time before a hockey game between the New York Rangers and the Philadelphia Flyers, an experience that led her to advocate "America the Beautiful" or "God Bless America" as the next national anthem. She told *The New York Times* sports columnist George Vecsey, when asked whether she was afraid of forgetting the words, "I'm an actress. I'm supposed to remember lines. They're also up there on the message board in case I need them. I've only blown it once, at a Cosmos game in New Jersey, when I sang, 'whose broad stars and bright stripes.' Don't know why I did it, but I did." Too bad there wasn't a message board in Lewiston, Maine, for Goulet.

Fans can be tough. A cheerleader for the Washington Redskins was booed when, given a chance to sing "The Star-Spangled Banner" before a football game, she botched the words. That led the Redskins' defensive back Deion

Sanders to say about the fans, "How can you boo a cheer-leader who's out there trying her precious little heart out to sing the national anthem? Half of them don't even know the words."

While some people draw inspiration every time they hear "The Star-Spangled Banner" played and others find it made meaningless by unending repetition, Robert Merrill is very definitely in the first group. "I'm the Star-Spangled Baritone!" the great opera singer and Yankee fan practi-cally shouted when I asked him about his extracurricular role as the singer of the national anthem at Yankee Sta-dium before baseball games. "I have sung it for thirty-two years with the Yankees—regular games, play-offs, World Series." In the early years, Merrill's performances were mostly live, but as he got older, recordings were used often.

How did this star of the Metropolitan Opera, known for his performances in *The Marriage of Figaro* and *Carmen*, get to be identified with the national anthem? "During World War Two, one of my first jobs was at the Roxy The-ater in New York," he said, "and someone asked me to record it to be played at every theater before the movie. God knows how many times it was heard." Now he is just as well known for singing at Yankee Stadium as at the Met. "When I leave Yankee Stadium," he said, "people say, 'There's the "O-say-can-you-see" guy!' At the Met, people say, 'Hey, Figaro!' 'Hey, Toreador!' "

What better person to ask about the difficulty of sing-ing "The Star-Spangled Banner" than the Metropolitan Opera star who sings at Yankee Stadium? "It does not

Robert Merrill, singing the national anthem before a Yankees game.

have an easy range for people who are not vocally trained," Merrill said. "Some interpretations bother me—rock or country singers—because you can't hear the melody."

Does he like "The Star-Spangled Banner?"

"Oh, yes, very much. But sometimes I do 'America the Beautiful.' They all sing along with me—fifty-two thousand the other day—and they applaud before I finish. It is very exciting. I wanted to be a Yankee when I was growing up in Brooklyn. When I was eight years old, I went to Yankee Stadium and saw Babe Ruth."

Yankee Stadium is cavernous, and sounds can echo back and forth. How does it affect Merrill's singing? It doesn't, he said. "I don't listen to it."

Merrill is one of those who advocate playing "The Star-

Paul Zimmerman, The Clocker

Spangled Banner" briskly, saying, "It should be done as a march."

Merrill said his fastest time for a performance of "The Star-Spangled Banner" was fifty seconds. How would he know that? It's because of Paul Zimmerman. Many sports fans know Zimmerman as a leading writer for *Sports Illustrated*, but I came upon him in a slightly different context. I was sitting in the press box in Robert F. Kennedy Stadium, covering a Washington Redskins football game, and when the national anthem started, I saw the beer commercials on the press-box television set and heard someone two rows in front of me yelling at the singer and the band (who, of course, couldn't hear him) to go faster, faster. Zimmerman, it turns out, has a stopwatch and has been timing performances of the national anthem for years.

This is his holy grail, to find performers to lower the performance times for "The Star-Spangled Banner." Other sportswriters in the past would have wanted to have been there when a runner pushed the time for the mile below four minutes for the first time or when a pitcher threw a perfect game in the World Series. Zimmerman longs for that national anthem below the magical fifty-second barrier. Why? If Merrill is inspired by "The Star-Spangled Banner," Zimmerman is bored by it.

Either Merrill misremembers, or he is exaggerating his stats like an old ballplayer, or he hit fifty seconds on a day that Zimmerman was absent, which, of course, would make his record unofficial since Zimmerman is the judge, jury and entire constituency of this event. "Merrill?" Zimmerman said. "He does one-ten to one-twenty like clockwork. Kind of snappy. It's decent. One night he did a one-seventeen and I told him, and he got annoyed. I told everyone the next day, 'Put your clock on him tonight.' That night he comes in at one-oh-six! He comes up to the press box and asks how he did. I tell him and he shoves his fist into the air and says, 'All right!' "

Zimmerman, who is the senior professional football writer for *Sports Illustrated* and is remembered by me and others from his days at the *New York Post*, ranges widely for his research. When I interviewed him, he said that he had timed "The Star-Spangled Banner" before 1,283 sports events, a precise figure that he offered with conviction as if to emphasize its verisimilitude. "John Kiley, the organist at Fenway Park, did it in fifty-one seconds in 1978 during the one-game playoff with the Yankees," Zimmerman said. "He once did a fifty-five even though he held the last note. 'Mr. Kiley,' I told him, 'I just wanted you to know that if you didn't hold that last note you had a chance of breaking my old record of fifty-three seconds set by the Princeton band in 1954 at the Columbia game.'" Zimmerman says he knows this because he was on the Columbia football team, a tackle on both offense and defense, and played in that game.

Kiley told Zimmerman that he had been criticized for playing the anthem too fast, but there is no such thing as a too-fast anthem for Zimmerman, who pressed Kiley to bear down, suck it up and go for the record. "He came in at fifty-one seconds!" Zimmerman said. "Fifty-one is the record. I told him, 'Mr. Kiley, I just want you to know that this is a big moment for me.' He said, 'I was thinking of you, son.'" The absolute fastest version that Zimmerman ever clocked was a breakneck forty-one seconds for the 1970 movie about the attack on Pearl Harbor, *Tora! Tora! Tora!,* in a shipboard scene. Zimmerman lists this record with an asterisk, like the apochryphal one given to Roger Maris when he broke Babe Ruth's home run record in 1961 during a longer season. And how did he clock this movie in the theater? Maybe his stopwatch glowed in the dark.

One of the longest performances, Zimmerman said, was by the legendary Pearl Bailey with two minutes twenty-eight seconds before a World Series game in 1978 or '79, and Leola Giles, a rock singer, once came in at a sultry two thirty-four.

Why does Zimmerman do this? "It's a crummy song and I want to get it over with as soon as possible," he said. "The national anthem is nothing but a question—O, say, can you see? It's not a good song. It's a pub song." He prefers "America the Beautiful" and "The Battle Hymn of the Republic."

It may not be a song loved by all, but it does stand as a pretty powerful symbol of our democracy. This is the story of how we got to this point.

2

The Widow, the Poet
and the Soldiers

In Philadelphia in 1776, in the city and the year of American independence, Mary Young was born into a family of flag makers. Her mother, Rebecca Flower Young, made a flag for George Washington during the revolution, and her brother, William Young, was also a flagmaker. So it is not surprising that Mary, now Mary Young Pickersgill, would be chosen in 1814 to make the huge flag that was needed to fly over Fort McHenry in Baltimore Harbor.

Mary Pickersgill's husband, John, was an English merchant she met in Baltimore. Widowed at a young age, she ran a successful business, a rare achievement for a woman in that male-dominated time. According to a history gathered by a Baltimore museum devoted to her great contribution, the Star-Spangled Banner Flag House: "An early account states that Mary was very popular in the society of her time, and her home was the scene of many gay entertainments. She was considered a woman of charm, culture and personality, vivacious and public spirited. She did not possess much wealth but was certainly part of the middle-class social structure." When she was named president of the Impartial Female Humane Society in 1851, she became the first woman to direct a charity in Baltimore. She died in Baltimore in 1857 at the age of eighty-one and deserves to be better known today.

Another of the principals in the story of the Star-Spangled Banner is very well known, a part of the legend and history of the United States—Francis Scott Key. He was virtually unknown before his moment of glory, his grand and lasting accomplishment, the writing of "The Star-Spangled Banner." His name is familiar today to every schoolchild, every American adult and, probably, every immigrant who has sworn allegiance to our nation and become a citizen. Before his grand moment, he was little known beyond his family, friends and colleagues in the Washington area, where he practiced law and dabbled in poetry. Key, who lived from 1780 to 1843, also served as United States attorney for the District of Columbia and he was a low-ranking officer during the War of 1812. He had been a mischievous schoolboy, given to the pranks that are part of growing up, and when he did reach adulthood he played a role in preserving his alma mater, and it is a good thing that he did. The school is St. John's College, in Annapolis, Maryland, which is today one of America's finest small colleges.

Lt. Col. George Armistead

There is one inescapable contradiction in Key's life. He owned slaves. He professed a strong Christian faith and yet he owned slaves. In each of the four verses of "The Star-Spangled Banner" there is the line "O'er the land of the free," but the man who wrote it owned slaves. Key's slaves worked his family farm, Terra Rubra, for the red clay there, in the western Maryland town of Frederick. That contradiction was one that Key had in common with many of the leaders of the Revolution, especially the large Virginia contingent that included George Washington, Thomas Jefferson and James Madison. They wrote and spoke eloquently of freedom, yet owned black people as their slaves.

The person who wound up linking the lives of Mary Young Pickersgill and Francis Scott Key was George Armistead. In June 1813, Armistead, then a major, arrived at Fort McHenry and soon told Major General Samuel Smith, the American commander in the area, "We, sir, are ready at Fort McHenry to defend Baltimore against invading by the enemy. This is to say, we are ready except that we have no suitable ensign to display over the Star Fort, and it is my desire to have a flag so large that the British will have no difficulty seeing it from a distance."

It was then that Mary Pickersgill received the order to make what became America's most famous flag.

These Americans have left their monuments. Key's, of course, is our national anthem. Pickersgill's monument is the flag that she made and Armistead's is Fort McHenry. There is another person in this story whose monument is of the more traditional sort, a piece of marble statuary among those of other British heroes in St. Paul's Cathedral in London. That statue honors the life and death of Major General Robert Ross, and if Pickersgill and Armistead are not known today, Ross is virtually invisible to Americans. Yet Ross played a major role in two of the best known events of the War of 1812—the burning of Washington and the unsuccessful attempt to capture Fort McHenry. Ross was killed during the British attack on Baltimore and an officer on the scene said that his death "seemed to have disorganized the whole plan of proceedings, and the fleet and army rested idle, like a watch without its mainspring." But for the death of Ross, the outcome of the attack on Baltimore might have been different. If the British had captured Baltimore, the outcome of the War of 1812 itself most likely would have been very different indeed.

3

★ ★ ★

The Second War of Independence

In 1807, the British were confident. Their main problem was with Napoleon. The feeling in England was that once he and his French army were dealt with, the greatest naval power that the world had ever seen would regard the Americans as little more than an annoyance, a mosquito to be swatted away. Despite the loss of its American colonies in the Revolutionary War, Britain still had an enormous empire that swept from Australia to India to Africa and to the Caribbean, with various points in between, including America's next-door neighbor, Canada.

Years later, in 1882, before he became a nationally known figure, Theodore Roosevelt blamed two early presidents, Thomas Jefferson and James Madison, for the weak military position of America during the early 1800s.

"It was criminal folly," Roosevelt wrote, "for Jefferson, and his follower Madison, to neglect to give us a force either of regulars or of well-trained volunteers during the twelve years they had in which to prepare for the struggle that anyone might see was inevitable." Roosevelt, a Republican, was happy to find fault with two presidents who were members of what evolved into the Democratic Party of TR's and our day. The Democrats, Roosevelt said, were "utterly helpless." His language sounds like that of today's Republicans accusing today's Democrats of neglecting the nation's defense. Jefferson and Madison were guilty of "ludicrous and painful folly and stupidity," Roosevelt said.

When Jefferson was reelected in 1804, America had a large merchant fleet that did a good business with both the British and the French while they fought each other. In fact, most of the goods that France depended on were carried aboard American ships. America had little in the way of a navy, and what it did have was so weak that pirates sailed not far offshore. When British warships began to stop American merchant ships with cargo headed to France, there was little that the United States could do about it. Little by little, the Americans and the British headed toward war with each other. The British were still disdainful of the United States, even though the Americans had, against all odds, already defeated the British once before. The young nation was confident. Indeed, America was overconfident.

On May 16, 1806, Britain proclaimed a blockade against shipping headed for France, requiring neutral ships to pay fees. The British wanted to make sure that no military goods were getting through. Napoleon countered the British blockade by declaring one of his own, putting the United States in an uncomfortable squeeze between the two great European powers. Then came another squeeze. The British retaliated against the French retaliation, saying that a neutral ship could not sail from one port to another if either was under French control.

Making matters worse for the Americans was the British contention that a British citizen could be seized by a British naval officer if found aboard the ship of another nation. This was no minor matter. Because American merchant ships paid higher wages than the British, and because conditions were better aboard American ships, many of the seamen aboard American ships were actually British sailors, frequently deserters from the King's navy. One estimate was that a quarter of the fifty thousand to one hundred thousand American seamen in the early nineteenth century were British, and thousands of them were seized by the British, solely on the ground of their supposed British citizenship. The United States maintained that any foreigner could become a citizen after five years of residence and after meeting some requirements. Britain insisted that anyone born British was British forever and maintained that it had the right to seize anyone aboard an American ship suspected of being British. Many British seamen had a reason other than economic for jumping ship—they had not volunteered for the navy in the first place but instead had been seized by impressment gangs and forced—even carried—aboard British ships.

No nation, certainly not the young and proud America, could tolerate this forever. Roosevelt wrote:

> Any innocent merchant vessel was liable to seizure at any moment; and when overhauled by a British cruiser short of men was sure to be stripped of most of her crew. The British officers were themselves the judges as to whether a seaman should be pronounced a native of America or of Britain, and there was no appeal from their judgment. If a captain lacked his full complement there was little doubt as to the view he would take of any man's nationality. The wrongs inflicted on our seafaring countrymen by their impressment into foreign ships formed the main cause of the war.

On June 1, 1807, Vice Admiral George Cranfield Berkeley, commander of the British ships along the American coast, declared that "many seamen, subjects of His Britannic Majesty, and serving in his ships and vessels," had deserted while on duty in the Chesapeake Bay and had joined the crew of an American ship, coincidentally also called the *Chesapeake*. If that weren't bad enough, the crewmen paraded openly on the streets of Norfolk, Virginia, "under the American flag," Berkeley fumed, and the city magistrates and American naval officers refused to give up the British seamen when the British insisted

British warship Leopard *(left) fires on American frigate*
Chesapeake, *1807.*

that they were deserters and demanded their return. Because of the refusal, Berkeley ordered British officers, should they ever come upon the *Chesapeake* at sea, to search the ship and seize any British deserters found aboard it. Berkeley added one fig leaf—if the captain of the *Chesapeake* wanted to search the British ship that stopped him to look for American deserters, he would be permitted to do so. Berkeley knew that the concession was meaningless—there would be no American deserters aboard the British ships.

The *Chesapeake*, a thirty-eight-gun frigate, had many British subjects among its crew, including at least four sailors from the British frigate *Melampus*, which had been patrolling off the American coast on the lookout for French shipping. The British demanded the return of the four, the

Americans refused and the *Chesapeake* set sail for the Mediterranean. On June 23, a British warship, the fifty-gun *Leopard*, caught up with the *Chesapeake* at sea and sent an officer aboard to demand that the British seamen be turned over. The American captain, Commodore James Barron, refused, and after forty-five minutes, the British officer returned to the *Leopard*. Here the accounts differ, depending on who is telling the story. The American version is that the *Leopard* suddenly fired on the *Chesapeake* without warning. The British version is that the commander of the *Leopard*, Captain Salusbury Humphreys, fired first a warning shot and then a broadside into the *Chesapeake*. The smaller *Chesapeake* returned a few ineffective rounds and the *Leopard* fired more broadsides into the *Chesapeake*, which took on five feet of water in her hold from the damage, forcing Barron to give up. The British seized the men it regarded as deserters—John Strawn, Daniel Martin, William Ware and John Wilson, according to the *Chesapeake*'s log, which indeed identified them as British deserters—and allowed the *Chesapeake* to sail on. The American ship returned to port. A British report said, "In this short encounter, the *Chesapeake* had six men killed and twenty-one wounded, and has returned into port very much shattered." The *Chesapeake*'s log put the number killed at three and named the dead as Joseph Arnold, Peter Shakely and John Lawrence, but it is possible that some men later died of their wounds and that the death toll of six is correct.

The lesson of the brief encounter was not lost on the

British. "As an aggressive enemy," *The Times* of London said, "America cannot, in its present divided state, be considered as formidable," the "divided state" referring to antiwar sentiment among Federalists in the Northeast and the more hawkish feelings in the South. And what of the supposed deserters? It was determined that three of them were Americans and the British offered to return them. The fourth was not so lucky. He was found to be a British subject and was summarily hanged, the harsh punishment traditionally meted out to deserters.

Americans were incensed by the British action, and although the United States was not in any position to oppose the British at sea, many called for retaliation. In Norfolk, Virginia, shortly after the incident, public meetings were called to express outrage and a mob burned two hundred water barrels belonging to the *Melampus*. The city barred any communication between the British consul in Norfolk and the British ships, and forbade the sale of food and water to British ships. On July 3, four British ships— *Bellona*, *Triumph*, *Leopard* and *Melampus*—anchored in Hampton Roads near Norfolk and an officer delivered a threatening note to the mayor of Norfolk from the commander of the British force, Commodore John E. Douglas. The letter said that the Norfolk action was "extremely hostile, not only in depriving the British Consul from discharging the duties of his office, but at the same time preventing me from obtaining that information so absolutely necessary for His Majesty's service."

"You must be aware," Douglas said ominously, "that

the British flag never has, nor will be insulted with impunity. You must also be aware, that it has been, and is still in my power, to obstruct the whole trade of the Chesapeake, since the late circumstance, which I desisted from, trusting that general unanimity would be restored. Respecting the circumstances of the deserters, lately apprehended from the United States frigate *Chesapeake*, that, in my opinion, must be decided between the two governments *alone*."

The Times of London on July 28, 1807, published an unsigned letter from Halifax, Nova Scotia, where Admiral Berkeley had his headquarters, that praised Humphreys for his coolness in the boarding of the *Chesapeake* and concluded, "What will be the result, time must determine; but if we give up the right of search, we shall soon be obliged to resign the empire of the seas."

The mayor of Norfolk, Richard E. Lee, answered Douglas's letter on July 4. Perhaps the patriotism of Independence Day encouraged the defiant tone of his opening words. "I have received your menacing letter of yesterday," wrote Lee, and he informed Douglas that "the American people are not to be intimidated by menace." He went on, "We do not seek hostility, nor shall we avoid it. We are prepared for the worst you may attempt, and will do whatever shall be judged proper to repel force, whensoever your efforts shall render any acts of ours necessary."

Easy enough for the mayor of Norfolk to threaten the British Empire, especially since he probably was not aware of how ill prepared the United States was at the time. The same attitude prevailed at an outdoor meeting in New York City under the chairmanship of DeWitt Clinton, later a governor of New York. That meeting declared its indignation at the attack by the *Leopard*, condemned it as being "in violation of our national rights" and called it a "fresh outrage offered to [our] National Sovereignty by the Navy of Great Britain."

"Although we cherish peace with the greatest sincerity," the meeting resolved, "yet . . . we hold ourselves ready, at the call of our Government, to resist all infringements of our national rights, and violation of our national honor."

The New Yorkers declared,

> Resolved, That we consider the dastardly and unprovoked attack made on the United States' armed ship *Chesapeake*, by his Britannic Majesty's ship *Leopard*, to be a violation of our national rights, as atrocious as it is unprecedented.

On the same day as the New York meeting, President Thomas Jefferson issued a proclamation in which he called the British action an outrage:

> A Frigate of the U.S. trusting to a state of peace, and leaving her Harbor on a distant service, has been surprised and attacked by a British Vessel of superior force, one of a squadron lying in our waters & covering the transaction, & has been disabled from

Service, with the loss of a number of men killed & wounded. This enormity was not only without provocation or justifiable cause, but was committed with the avowed purpose of taking by force from a ship of war of the United States a part of her crew, and that no circumstances might be wanting to mark its character, it had been previously ascertained that the seamen thus forcibly seized, demanded were native Citizens of the U.S. Having effected her purpose, she returned to anchor with her squadron within our jurisdiction.

War, for which America was not prepared and which the British wanted to avoid so they could concentrate on fighting Napoleon and the French, was put off after the British apologized, disavowed Berkeley's actions and offered to pay reparations. Yet the damage had been done. The British made a show of removing Berkeley from his command in Halifax, but the Americans did not regard the action as genuine since Berkeley was simply given a different command and his career did not suffer. One American casualty of the *Chesapeake* affair was Commodore Barron, the ship's captain, who was found guilty of neglect and suspended from command. The *Chesapeake* was an unlucky ship. On June 1, 1813, it was defeated in a battle off Boston by the British frigate *Shannon*. The cannon fire and hand-to-hand combat were ferocious. American losses were seventy killed and one hundred wounded, while the British had thirty-three dead and fifty wounded. Among the American dead was the *Chesapeake*'s captain, James Lawrence, who became famous after his death for his last command to his crew, "Don't give up the ship!"

At Jefferson's request, Congress passed an embargo act in December 1807, hoping that withdrawing American goods from the British and French would force them to treat the United States with more respect. It had the effect of causing an economic depression as well as a temporary revival of the Federalists. American farmers, in particular, suffered, while smugglers prospered. The American attempt to force respect from Britain without going to war failed and the embargo was repealed in March 1809.

This American bellicosity was not nationwide. The Federalists, who were strongest in New England, opposed going to war with Britain. The Federalists were in decline and would soon disappear from the American scene, but the British saw them as possible sympathizers and, when war did come, generally left New England alone.

What little the United States had in the way of a navy was put on a hair trigger because of the *Chesapeake* affair. Commodore John Rodgers, the commander of a squadron patrolling the coast, received a warning from the secretary of the navy, Paul Hamilton, that "what has been perpetrated may be again attempted." Transmitting that warning to his captains, Rodgers added:

> Every man, woman, and child, in our country, will be active in assigning our names to disgrace, and even the very vessels composing our little navy

to the ravages of worms, or the detestable transmigration to merchantmen, should we not fulfil their expectations. I should consider the firing of a shot by a vessel of war, of either nation, and particularly England, at one of our public vessels, whilst the colors of her nation are flying on board of her, as a menace of the grossest order, and in amount an insult which it would be disgraceful not to resent by the return of two shots at least; while should the shot strike, it ought to be considered an act of hostility meriting chastisement to the utmost extent of all your force.

The tiny American navy would not go down without a fight.

In the next major naval incident leading up to the War of 1812, it was an American ship that got the better of the British vessel, although there is some question as to who fired first. Again, the underlying cause was Britain invoking what it insisted was its right to take British seamen from American ships at sea. In May 1811 the British cruiser *Guerrière* was sailing off the New Jersey coast about eighteen miles from New York City, overtook a small American coastal brig, the *Spitfire*, and carried off a member of its crew. It turned out that the crewman was an American citizen, a native of Maine, and an American frigate, the forty-four-gun *President*, which was cruising in the same waters, took off in pursuit of the *Guerrière*. The *President*'s commander was Commodore Rodgers, who earlier had warned his officers against allowing the American navy to be dishonored in battle. While the *President* sailed south in search of the *Guerrière*, a British ship in the *Guerrière*'s group, a corvette called the *Little Belt*, spotted the *President* on May 16 and, thinking it was the *Guerrière*, headed toward it.

The ships were in the Atlantic Ocean forty or fifty miles off Cape Henry, Virginia. The *President* spotted the *Little Belt*, a twenty-gun ship much smaller than the *Guerrière*, and sailed toward it. Both the American and British ships thought they were approaching the *Guerrière*, and both were wrong. The British mistake was a fatal one. Commander Arthur Bingham, captain of the *Little Belt*, sometimes known as the *Lille Belt*, finally realized the ship he was approaching was not the *Guerrière* and turned about, trying to get away. The *President*, thinking it was chasing the *Guerrière*, caught up with the *Little Belt*, but by that time it was 8:00 P.M. and darkness had fallen. Bingham said later that he prepared his guns for action and hoisted his colors so that the American ship would "see what we were." As Bingham described the uneven battle, "He came within hail, I hailed & asked what ship it was, he repeated my questions, I again hailed & asked what ship it was. He again repeated my words and fired a broadside, which I instantly returned, the action then became general & continued for three-quarters of an hour, when she ceased firing and appeared to be on fire about the main hatchway." When finally the two captains could make themselves heard to each other, the American captain,

American frigate President *(left) attacks British sloop of war* Little Belt, *1811.*

Commodore Rodgers, asked if he could send a boat to the *Little Belt* and Bingham said he could. According to Bingham, Rodgers sent a message saying that "he lamented much the unfortunate affair (as he termed it) that had happened, and that had he known our force was so inferior he should not have fired on me."

"I asked his motive for having fired at all," the British captain said, "his reply was that we fired the first gun at him, which was positively not the case." Bingham said that he had ordered his crew not to fire first and pointed out that it would have been rather foolish for his smaller vessel to have fired at the American frigate. An American naval court of inquiry ruled that the British ship had fired first, accepting Rodgers's statement that shots of thirty-two-pound cannonballs from the *Little Belt* had cut away rigging and damaged the mainmast. After the battle, the Americans offered to help the *Little Belt* to a port in the United States, an offer Bingham said he immediately declined.

"I have to lament the loss of thirty-two men killed & wounded among whom the Master," Commander Bingham wrote in his official report, an accurate counting of the casualties but one that has the effect of exaggeration since the toll of thirty-two consisted of nine dead and twenty-three wounded. Bingham went on: "His Majesty's ship is much damaged in her masts, sails, rigging & hull, and there are many shots thro' between wind and water & many shot still remaining in her side and upper works all shot away, starboard pump also, I have judged it proper to proceed to Halifax."

Rodgers had a different description of the battle. The *Little Belt*, he said, did not fly its colors, which meant that he did not know its nationality. It was getting dark during the chase, Rodgers said, and in the twilight he took the ship to be the *Guerrière*, saying later that it gave him great pain at the end of the battle to discover that he had engaged a much smaller ship. The *Little Belt*, he said, seemed to be taking evasive action and the *President* caught up to within one hundred yards. Rodgers wrote in his official report:

I hailed "What ship is that?" to this enquiry no answer was given, but I was hailed by her commander & asked "What ship is that?" Having asked the first question, & of course considering myself entitled by the common rules of politeness to the first answer, after a pause of fifteen or twenty seconds, I reiterated my first enquiry of "What ship is that?" & before I had time to take the trumpet from my mouth, was answered by a shot that cut off one of our Maintopmast breast back stay's & went into our Main Mast, at this instant Capt Caldwell who was standing very near to me on the gangway having observed "Sir, she has fired on us" caused me to pause for a moment just as I was in the act of giving an order to fire a shot in return: & before I had time to resume the repetition of the intended order, a shot was actually fired from the second division of this ship; & was scarcely out of the gun, before it was answered from our assumed enemy by three others in quick succession; & soon after the rest of his broadside & musketry.

Rodgers said he initially thought that the first shot fired from the *Little Belt* might have been set off in error and so fired only a single shot in return. But the following British volley made plain that there had been no accident and that the British action was "violating our neutrality & insulting our Flag." Rodgers gave the order to return fire and in four to six minutes the *Little Belt*'s guns were silenced. It was only then, Rodgers said, that he realized that the *Little Belt* was so much smaller than his *President*. The captain said later that while he regretted the loss of life aboard the *Little Belt* and the great damage done to the British ship, he had had no choice but to respond to the "insult to the Flag of my Country." The *President* suffered little damage, most of it limited to the rigging and mast. No Americans were killed and just one member of the crew, a boy, was wounded. The secretary of the navy, Paul Hamilton, responded to Rodgers with praise, saying his actions had earned him esteem and respect, and he asked the name of the wounded boy so that he could promote him to midshipman. Eventually, Rodgers was exonerated in an official investigation by a naval board of inquiry and President James Madison let it be known that he approved of Rodgers's action. The British later adopted the American finding as well, but American hostility to the British and overconfidence in American military might rose further.

The *Guerrière* had another role to play in the War of 1812. On August 19, 1812, the American navy's most famous ship, the *Constitution*, attacked the *Guerrière* off Cape Race, Newfoundland. The *Guerrière* suffered so much damage that its captain surrendered the ship to the Americans. So many cannon shots from the *Guerrière* bounced harmlessly off the *Constitution*'s hull that the crew nicknamed the ship Old Ironsides, a name that has remained to this day with the vessel, now on display in Boston.

The *New York Evening Post,* its writer still reflecting the

earlier mistaken assumption that the *President* had encountered the *Guerrière*, the vessel that had taken off the American seaman, said of the encounter of the *President* and the
Little Belt:

> The event itself has excited a sensation perfectly
> decisive of the wishes and the feelings of the na-
> tion, on the subjects of our flag and our impressed
> citizens—not a man of any party (unless a few Brit-
> ish agents, to whom our honor and interests are
> both objects of anguish) has expressed a sentiment,
> but such as renders credit to Commodore Rodgers,
> and such as goes to sustain the Government, if it
> will but sustain the rights of the nation and its citi-
> zens throughout.
>
> *She Stoops to Conquer, or the Mistakes of a Night, a*
> *new play with an old title*, was performed with loud ap-
> plause on Thursday evening, the 16th instant, off
> the Capes of Virginia, by the frigate *President*, and a
> British picaroon, to the gratification of *all* America.
> The British picaroon, whose rashness Commodore
> Rogers chastised, is suspected to be the same *man-*
> *stealer* that kidnapped a young American on board
> the *Spitfire*, about a fortnight since, as she was
> entering the port of New York.

There were war cries on both sides of the Atlantic.
One eyewitness account of the *President–Little Belt* encounter, from a British sailor aboard the *President*, pro-

vided anti-American ammunition to any British subjects who needed it. The account came from William Burket, who said that he was born in Deptford, England, and went to sea at the age of twenty in 1808, first to Montego Bay, Jamaica, and then to New York City aboard a brig called the *Pizarro* in 1809. While in New York, "being in a state of intoxication," according to his account, Burket said that he was forcibly carried on board the American armed schooner *Revenge*, then later transferred to the *President*. While the ship was in Annapolis, Maryland, he said, word came of the boarding of an American brig by a British ship, presumably the *Spitfire* by the *Guerrière*, and the *President* took on a large quantity of ammunition and headed out to sea to search for the *Guerrière*. When the *President* got within pistol range of a vessel that turned out to be the *Little Belt*, Burket said, Commodore Rodgers ordered his crew not to fire until ordered to do so, but a gun aboard the *President* was fired, by accident, Burket believed.

The next thing he knew, the *President* fired a broadside at the *Little Belt* and although "not a gun had been fired" by the *Little Belt*, the *President* "continued firing about half an hour without cessation." Burket (whose name is also given as Burkit) gave his account to justices of the peace in Halifax, Nova Scotia, and he clearly had good reason to give statements agreeable to the British, to whose jurisdiction he had returned, and the account was printed prominently in *The Times* of London. His statement concluded:

This deponent further saith, that the crew of the *President* consists of about five hundred men, upwards of three hundred of which he knows to be British seamen, from having conversed with them, and having heard them declare they were so, and from many of them having designated the places they came from; that the engagement with the *Little Belt* had excited great disgust in the British seamen on board the *President*, who had manifested their reluctance to fight against their country; that one man in particular had so plainly expressed this feeling, as to have drawn on him the resentment of Commodore Rodgers, who had him put in irons; in which situation he remained when this deponent left the ship for the aforesaid offense, and for having said that the first gun was fired from the *President*.

This deponent further saith, that, after the *President* came into New-York, and was lying in the North River, that by the assistance of his hammock lashings, he got in the night from the fore-chains into the river, and swam to a place of safety, and has since procured a passage to Halifax.

John Russell, another sailor aboard the *President*, who probably was British, gave a similar account in Bristol, England:

John Russell deposes, that he belonged to the *President* American frigate; that he did his duty in the fore-top; was quartered at the aftermost gun on the forecastle, before they fell in with the *Little Belt*. The Commodore informed the ship's company, that he was ordered to demand two American seamen that had been pressed by a British frigate; if they were not gived up, he was to take them by force; when they went down to the *Little Belt* the guns were double-shotted and loaded with grape; that the first gun was fired from the *President*, but he believes by accident, as no orders were given from the quarter-deck to fire; the guns had locks, and were all cocked. After the action, he was informed by the men in the waste, that a man was entangled with the lanyard of the lock, that occasioned the gun to go off.

In those early days of the Republic, Congress did not meet year-round as it does now, and the encounter of the *President* and the *Little Belt* occurred while Congress was not in session. It is so hot in Washington during the summer that it took the invention of air-conditioning many years later to permit Congress to meet year-round. Whether this is good or bad for the republic is subject to debate. On July 24, 1811, President James Madison summoned Congress to meet on November 4, a month ahead of schedule, and when it convened Madison told the Senate and the House of Representatives that the United States could not tolerate attacks on the sovereignty that it had won in its War of Independence. Madison was reluctant, but the nation was headed toward another war with Britain, a conflict that has been called the Second War of Independence. Of course, that is a bit of an exaggeration, since the British had long since given up any hope of recovering the colonies. Madison asked Congress to increase the military force, and the tone of the debate openly anticipated war with Britain. At the time, an army of ten thousand was authorized but, in fact, only five thousand were in the ranks. Congress approved filling the army to the ten-thousand level and to add twenty-five thousand more to the regular army as well as fifty thousand volunteers (equivalent to members of today's National Guard), although many expressed doubts that enough recruits could be found to reach those levels.

There were other causes for the war that was soon to come, including the notion that the United States should expand into Canada, which many Americans thought could be taken easily from Britain. One member of the House of Representatives, Felix Grundy of Tennessee, said that Canada ought to be annexed by America so that the North could retain the balance that it had with the South but was bound to lose when the recently acquired Louisiana gained population. Some advocated war on the ground that victories would weaken the Indian nations allied with Britain, thereby making Indian lands open to white expansion, while others saw it as a way of annexing Florida, which was held by Spain, Britain's ally. Henry Clay of Kentucky, one of the great leaders in the history of the House, urged war as the only way to get the British to revoke the Orders in Council, which were issued against the United States on November 11, 1807, and restricted American trade. Clay also saw Canada as an inviting target because it gave shelter to Indian allies of the British. Speaking of Canada, Clay said, "Other gentlemen consider the invasion of that country as wicked and unjustifiable. Its inhabitants are represented as unoffending, connected with those of the bordering States by a thousand tender ties, interchanging acts of kindness, and all the offices of good neighborhood. Canada innocent! Canada unoffending! Is it not in Canada that the tomahawk of the savage has been molded into its deathlike form?" Another of the great leaders of Congress, John C. Calhoun of South Carolina, was also a strong advocate of war, aligned with members of Congress known as "war hawks."

Should the United States give in to the British? Clay asked in another debate. His answer: "Who ever learned, in the school of base submission, the lessons of noble freedom, and courage, and independence?"

Madison had been reluctant to go to war against the British, writing to Jefferson on April 24, 1812, "At present, great differences of opinion exist as to the time and form of entering into hostilities; whether at a very early or later day." But in the end he felt he had no choice and on June 1 sent a war message to Congress. In his message, Madison wrote of the British insistence on seizing crewmen from ships of other nations. "The practice, hence, is so far from affecting British subjects alone that, under the pretext of searching for those, thousands of American citizens, under the safeguard of public law and of their national flag, have been torn from their country and from everything dear to them; have been dragged on board ships of war of a foreign nation and exposed, under the severities of their discipline, to be exiled to the most distant and deadly climes, to risk their lives in the battles of their oppressors, and to be the melancholy instruments of taking away those of their own brethren."

The result was a declaration of war against Britain, with the Federalists opposing. The House voted for war on June 4 by seventy-nine to forty-nine and the Senate voted for it on June 17 by nineteen to thirteen, with President Madison signing the declaration the next day. The vote was along sectional lines, with most from the South, the West and Pennsylvania voting for it and most from the rest of the North and East against it. That also reflected the geographical breakdown of the parties. Most of the Republicans (Madison's party, today's Democrats) voted for war; all of the Federalists voted against. Five days after Madison signed the declaration of war, the British government canceled its Orders in Council, but since the only way that word could be spread between the United States and Great Britain was by a long voyage, the American war vote and the British cancellation passed each other at sea. Had there been a transatlantic cable, not available until 1858, war might have been averted. Madison later wrote that war might have been put off, or "stayed," as he put it, had he heard promptly of the cancellation, but, of course, there was no cable and no way then that he could have known of it. Thus the war was fought after one of its main causes had been removed.

Woodrow Wilson, like Theodore Roosevelt a historian before being elected president, wrote, "It was a foolhardy and reckless risk the Congress was taking." One of the first actions of the government was to order General William Hull, the commander of the American forces in Michigan, to invade Canada. The assumption was that Canadians would flock to the Americans and join the United States. The war would be over soon, many thought. They were wrong.

4

***

Why the British Burned Washington and Other War Stories

The French were actually interfering more with American trade than were the British, but Britain was the more inviting target because of the British seizure of sailors on American ships, the possibility that Canada could be conquered and made part of the United States, and attempts by the British to enlist Indians as their allies. Many Americans old enough to remember the Revolutionary War recalled America's close relationship with the French, who had been an important ally in that war. That kinship was deepened when the French, drawing at least some inspiration from the Americans, overthrew their king in their own revolution. Woodrow Wilson wrote, "The country, as if by hereditary choice, chose to fight England and let France go her way for the present." The real enemy, as

44

Wilson later saw it, was the French emperor. "Napoleon was the enemy of the civilized world, had been America's own enemy in disguise, and had thrown off the disguise," Wilson said. "England was fighting him almost alone, all Europe thrown into his scale and hers almost kicking the beam; and now America had joined the forces of Napoleon, in fact if not in intention, as he had subtly planned. It was natural that the raw and rural nation should thus have seen its own interests in isolation and indulged its own passion of resentment and selfishness. England's policy had cut America to the quick and had become intolerable." Wilson summed things up: "It was a tragical but natural accident that the war should be against England, not against France."

Years earlier, Thomas Jefferson had said much the same thing, but being Jefferson, he'd said it more eloquently, more concisely: "England seems to have become a den of pirates and France a den of thieves."

The war got under way in what would look today like slow motion. While the Americans declared war in June 1812, it took the British six months to get around to its own declaration. Although many Americans regarded it as the Second War of Independence, the British did not seriously contemplate trying to recover their former colonies. On the contrary, they were at a loss as to how to fight a war along a coastline fifteen hundred miles long and separated from them by an ocean. Even after they declared war, it took the British eighteen months more to assemble an expeditionary force, although British troops based in Canada engaged in battle well before the official declaration.

The British government declared war on January 9, 1813, blaming the Americans for starting a war over disputes that it said were trivial or negotiable. The declaration made clear that the seizure of supposed British citizens from American ships remained an important issue. The declaration of war said that "the President of the United States has, it is true, since proposed to Great Britain an armistice," but that this was "on condition that Great Britain, as a preliminary step, should do away [with] a cause of war, now brought forward for the first time— namely, that she should abandon the exercise of her undoubted right of search, to take from American merchant vessels British seamen, the natural-born subjects of His Majesty."

The declaration went on: "There is no right more clearly established than the right which a Sovereign has to the allegiance of his subjects, more especially in time of war. Their allegiance is no optional duty, which they can decline and resume at pleasure. It is a call which they are bound to obey: it began with their birth, and can only terminate with [the end of] their existence." The asserted right of America to impart United States citizenship on British subjects was a "novel pretension" of the Americans that, if allowed to stand, would "expose to danger the very foundation of our maritime strength," the British said. Finally, toward the end of the war declaration, the British government got to what it saw as the real underlying cause, saying, "But the real origin of the present contest will be found in that spirit which has long unhappily actuated the councils of the United States: their marked partiality in palliating and assisting the aggressive tyranny of France."

The British added, "From their common origin, from their common interests, from their professed principles of freedom and independence, the United States were the last power in which Great Britain could have expected to find a willing instrument and abettor of French tyranny."

When the war began, the British had a much larger navy than the United States, consisting of six hundred warships, although not all of them could be sent to American waters because of expected battles in Europe. The United States had just sixteen ships, and none of them were as big as the first-line British ships. On land, the United States had about eighteen thousand army troops, outnumbering the seven thousand British and Canadian soldiers in Canada.

Things quickly went badly for the Americans. The British captured Mackinac Island in the Michigan Territory on July 17, 1812. Fort Dearborn—now Chicago—was abandoned to the Indian allies of the British on August 15. The next day, the Americans surrendered Detroit with twenty-five hundred taken prisoner. The loss of Detroit was particularly galling. Brigadier General William Hull, the governor of the Michigan Territory, was commander of the American forces in the region, and he had served with distinction in the Revolutionary War. A force of about fifteen hundred British and Indian troops led by Major General Isaac Brock surrounded Detroit and demanded that Hull surrender, which he did, effectively turning over all of Michigan to the British.

The war was tragic for both generals. Brock was killed in October 1812 by American forces invading Canada, and Hull, who was made the scapegoat by higher-ups who had assigned him a difficult task but failed to provide enough troops, was court-martialed in 1814, convicted of cowardice and sentenced to be shot. He was spared execution when President James Madison granted him a pardon because of his Revolutionary War service.

The War of 1812 marked the only time that the United States was ever invaded by a foreign power, but the invasion was largely in retaliation for the American attack on Canada. Instead of marching into Canada and conquering it, the Americans were in retreat. The American navy, which should have been a real underdog to the British, on the other hand, did better, winning the first five one-on-one battles. Eventually, the British navy shut down American ports, curtailing imports and exports with its blockades.

On April 27, 1813, Captain Isaac Chauncey led an American naval squadron of fourteen vessels in an attack on York, now Toronto, the capital of Upper Canada. According to a nineteenth-century American account, the area was once known as Tarontah, an Indian word that means "trees on the water." When the French built a fort there, they called it Fort Tarontah, which evolved into

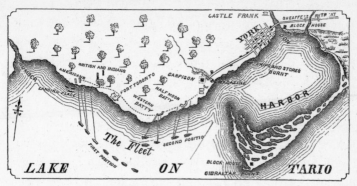

American and British positions during the attack on York, Ontario (present-day Toronto).

Toronto. When the British took over the area, it was re-named York in honor of a son of King George III. It later reverted to Toronto. Dr. Carl Benn, chief curator of the City of Toronto Museum and Heritage Services, differs with that version. He says that *Toronto* derives from a term that means "fish weirs" and actually refers to a site more than sixty miles north of the city that was placed at its current location by a seventeenth-century map maker's mistake.

Chauncey's ships bombarded the shoreline west of the town to prevent the British troops from forming properly while sixteen hundred troops under Brigadier General Zebulon Pike went ashore. Pike had earlier discovered what came to be known as Pikes Peak while on an explo-ration for President Thomas Jefferson after the Louisiana Purchase. In the attack, Pike and 37 of his men were killed, with 222 wounded, when a powder magazine blew up. The death of the general had a consequence that could not have been guessed then—the burning of Washington later in the war and the subsequent attack on Baltimore that brought us "The Star-Spangled Banner." This came about because the American troops went on a rampage, either to avenge the death of Pike or because they were undisciplined and their officers were unable or unwilling to control them. They burned down many structures, including the buildings that housed the provincial government—the Parliament Building in York and the Governor's House at Fort York. The Americans set fire to the government buildings despite an agreement in the surrender not to do so, and the British returned the favor when they captured Washington and put to the torch the equivalent American buildings, the Capitol and the White House.

One account tells the story that the British commander at York, Major General Sir Roger Hale Sheaffe, ordered that the gunpowder magazine in the fort be blown up to prevent the Americans from seizing the gunpowder and munitions stored there. The debris from the explosion soared into the air and fell on the Americans, killing or wounding more than 250, including Pike.

The American occupation of York lasted for six days, and according to Dr. Carl Benn, it was an ugly affair. Despite the terms of surrender, houses and businesses were looted by American soldiers. A large quantity of wine and liquor was stolen, the printing press of *The York Gazette* was destroyed, and the library and church were robbed. The provincial parliament buildings, the clerks' offices, the town blockhouse and General Sheaffe's house were burned, and the Americans released the inmates of the town jail, some of whom joined in the pillaging.

Revenge was demanded by many residents of York, who were joined later in that cry by the people of Niagara, then called Newark, when their town was also torched in December 1813 by the Americans, who also set parts of the neighboring town of Queenston on fire. Sir George Prevost, the British governor-in-chief of Canada, asked one of the naval leaders, Vice-Admiral Sir Alexander Cochrane, to punish the Americans, saying that he should "assist in inflicting that measure of retaliation which shall deter the enemy from a repetition of similar outrages." Cochrane then ordered his officers to carry out retaliatory acts in the United States, telling them, "You are hereby required and directed to destroy and lay waste such towns and districts as you may find assailable. You will hold strictly in view the conduct of the American army towards His Majesty's unoffending Canadian subjects, and you will spare merely the lives of the unarmed American inhabitants of the United States. For only by carrying this retaliation into the country of our enemy can we hope to make him sensible of the impolicy as well as the inhumanity of the system he has adopted."

It was clear that the British burned Washington in retaliation for the American burning of Toronto, but that cause is virtually unknown to Americans today. Why?

Carl Benn gave this answer, which he characterized as an outsider's view.

"I believe that Americans don't like to be the bad guys and don't like to lose. In the case of the War of 1812, they were the bad guys who tried to conquer Canada, and they lost. The popular view among Americans is that they saw themselves going to war over naval rights and that the war was mostly fought on the sea, with some land battles in Washington, Baltimore and New Orleans. We used to have a survey to ask visitors to Historic Fort York what was the most surprising thing that they learned here, and eighty percent of the Americans said, 'I never knew we invaded Canada.' This is hardly a surprise: they tend to know very little about Canada and there is a strong propaganda quality to American history in the U.S. I don't think there's another western democracy that abuses its history to affirm a nation's 'goodness' as much as the United States does. From our side of the border, it's all very amusing."

By autumn, the Americans had decided to postpone their attempts at capturing Canada and withdrew to Plattsburg, New York, for the winter, a move approved of by a thirty-five-year-old lawyer who lived near Washington, Francis Scott Key, who objected to the war on religious grounds. It was not until later in the war, when British troops threatened the Chesapeake, that Key joined the militia.

By 1814, the Americans had lost their chance to take Canada, because Napoleon was finally defeated in April and the British could turn their full attention to the United States. The British began their campaign with a series of raids on towns in Maryland and Virginia. First came Leonardtown, Maryland, where an American regiment quickly withdrew on July 19, followed by Nomini Ferry in Virginia two days later. In the next three weeks, the British met little resistance as they rumbled through the countryside, attacking at St. Clements Creek, Maryland; Machodoc Creek, Virginia, and Hamburgh and Chaptico on the Wicomico River in Maryland. Next the British defeated the Americans at Kinsale, Virginia, and after a few more raids, they withdrew, having destroyed or captured American ships, seized food, tobacco and other supplies, and blown up or burned fortifications.

On August 19, British troops landed at Benedict, Maryland, on the Patuxent River, a tributary of the Chesapeake Bay. The British naval force was on the Patuxent because its goal was to destroy an American flotilla there under the command of Commodore Joshua Barney, a hero of the American Revolution, but the larger British ships could not go beyond Benedict because the river was too shallow. While the larger vessels put their troops ashore, the smaller British ships pursued the American force, and Barney, trapped in the upper reaches of the river, destroyed his sixteen vessels and landed his four hundred sailors to join the American army forces that were being assembled to block a British march on Washington, just twenty miles away.

The British, amazed that they were meeting such little

resistance, advanced toward Washington, which was lightly guarded because the American government did not regard it as much of a military target. Strictly speaking, the government was correct because Washington was a small, swampy town without much in the way of military facilities and it had just 8,208 people in the 1810 census, although nearby Alexandria, Virginia, had 7,227 people and Georgetown 4,948. What the Americans had failed to take into account was the attractiveness of Washington as a symbolic target, the locus of revenge for the sacking by the Americans of York in Canada. At an emergency cabinet meeting called by President Madison on July 1, Secretary of War John Armstrong insisted that Washington was not at risk because the main target of the British was Baltimore. On their way to the capital, the greatest difficulty encountered by the British came from the oppressive August heat of the Washington area. A young British officer wrote in his journal, "I do not recollect a period of my life when I suffered more severely from heat and fatigue; and . . . before many hours had elapsed, numbers of men began to fall behind, from absolute inability to keep up." Anyone who has spent an August in Washington will understand this. A more senior officer, Colonel Arthur Brooke, wrote in his diary, "Our poor fellows being so tired from the long march of the morning, and the excessive heat of the day, that many of them in striving to keep up fell down from actual fatigue, and breathed their last."

Meanwhile, a company of one hundred American soldiers camped out on the north lawn of the White House

OF THE WAR OF 1812.

Battle-ground at Bladensburg.

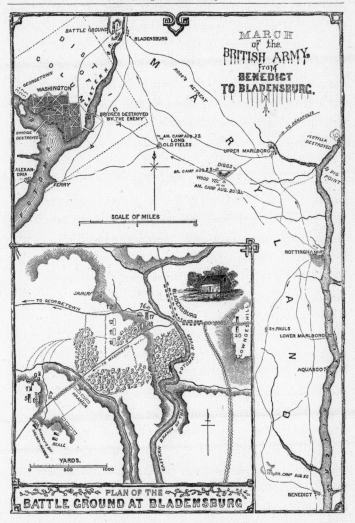

PLAN OF THE
BATTLE GROUND AT BLADENSBURG

and cannon were mounted there for its defense. State papers were taken across the Potomac River for safekeeping in Virginia and on August 24, the British force reached Bladensburg, Maryland, just five miles from the White House. Bladensburg is on the Eastern Branch of the Potomac, now known as the Anacostia River, and it was there that the Americans attempted to make a stand. The British invasion force numbered five thousand, but only fifteen hundred soldiers, sailors, marines and freed slaves were on the lines as they attacked a force of eight thousand Americans. However, the Americans were poorly equipped, poorly led and poorly organized, many of them citizens organized into militia units. The militia from Georgetown, then a separate community but now a neighborhood of modern Washington, was led by Brigadier General Walter Smith, who described his troops as "all volunteers of comfortable station." Smith was a lay leader of St. John's Episcopal Church in Georgetown, and a number of militia members were from St. John's, including Francis Scott Key, whose opposition to the war ended when the British landed on American soil. Key was among those who faced the well-drilled British troops. The battle began at 1:00 P.M. and ended in three hours, with the Americans thoroughly defeated and put to flight. Most of the British force paused for a while at Bladensburg to recover from the heat and the battle, while Major General Robert Ross, the British army commander, took a reserve force on the road to Washington.

President Madison had witnessed the Battle of Bladensburg and, before fleeing himself at 2:00 P.M., sent his messenger, James Smith, a free black man, to ride to the White House with an order for his wife, Dolley, to flee. She was fearful but outwardly calm. Years later, Dolley Madison wrote in a re-creation of that day, "I am accordingly ready. I have pressed as many Cabinet papers into trunks as to fill one carriage. . . . I am determined not to go myself until I see Mr. Madison safe. . . . I hear of much hostility towards him. Disaffection stalks around us. My friends and acquaintances are all gone." She forbade spiking the cannon at the north lawn with an explosion because she feared that would panic the residents of Washington. The dinner table would be set as if nothing untoward were happening—in fact, the table was set for forty people—and ale, cider and wine were brought up from the White House cellar. By midafternoon, Smith galloped up the White House drive and shouted that everyone should flee. "Clear out!" he cried. Dolley Madison insisted that the portrait of George Washington by Gilbert Stuart be taken down, lest it fall into British hands, and so it was saved and hangs today in the White House. Stephen Pleasonton, a senior clerk, removed the Declaration of Independence and sent it to safety, hiding it in a gristmill. Amid all this confusion, servants continued dinner preparations, including decanting wine into cut-glass bottles on the sideboard. Finally Mrs. Madison left, heading for the safety of Virginia, though an hour later the thoroughly discouraged President Madison returned to the White House and poured himself a glass of wine.

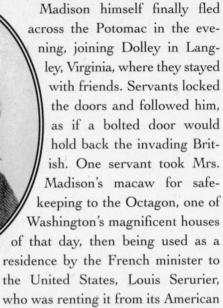

James Madison

Madison himself finally fled across the Potomac in the evening, joining Dolley in Langley, Virginia, where they stayed with friends. Servants locked the doors and followed him, as if a bolted door would hold back the invading British. One servant took Mrs. Madison's macaw for safekeeping to the Octagon, one of Washington's magnificent houses of that day, then being used as a residence by the French minister to the United States, Louis Serurier, who was renting it from its American owner. Serurier sent a message to General Ross, asking that the Octagon house be spared destruction since it was the French embassy, and it was not destroyed. Later, after the British burned Washington and left for Baltimore, Serurier moved his embassy to Philadelphia and the owner of the Octagon house, John Tayloe III, invited the Madisons to live there while the White House was restored. The Madisons lived there from September 1814 to March 1815. The Octagon house would have one more role to play in the War of 1812—Madison signed the Treaty of Ghent there on February 17, 1815, ending the conflict.

General Ross and his British navy counterpart, Rear Admiral George Cockburn, took Bladensburg quickly and set out for Washington, arriving on the evening of August 24, 1814. Bent on carrying out Admiral Cochrane's orders to punish the Americans for burning York, they quickly put the city's public buildings to the torch. First to be set afire was the Capitol, but not before the British had a bit of fun. Admiral Cockburn sat in the Speaker's chair in the House of Representatives and asked, "Shall this harbor of Yankee democracy be burned? All for it say aye!" The resolution carried and the deed was done, and then a force of 150 men set out down Pennsylvania Avenue to the White House. They broke into it and found the set dinner table, and the officers enjoyed the food and wine while the lower ranks prepared to burn the building. General Ross wrote in a letter—Jonathan referring to the Americans and John Bull the British—"So unexpected was our entry and capture of Washington, and so confident was Madison of the defeat of our troops, that he had prepared a supper for the expected conquerors; and when our advanced party entered the President's house they found a table laid with forty covers. The fare, however, which was intended for Jonathan, was voraciously devoured by John Bull, and the health of the Prince Regent, and success to His Majesty's arms by sea and land, was drunk in the best wines, Madison having taken to his heels, and ensured his safety on the opposite bank of the river by causing the bridge to be broken down." Rags soaked in oil were lit and the White House went up in flames.

Besides the White House, which was then called the President's House as it had not yet gotten its coat of white

CAPTURE AND BURNING OF WASHINGTON BY THE BRITISH, IN 1814.

The burning of the President's House by British soldiers.

paint, and the Capitol, the British burned the Treasury, the War Department building, an arsenal and American war supplies. The Library of Congress was then housed in the Capitol and lost its collection of 3,000 books in the fire. The library was reestablished in 1815 when Thomas Jefferson sold it his personal library of 6,487 books for $23,950, the equivalent of more than $217,000 in today's money.

The Americans burned the Washington Navy Yard to prevent it from falling into British hands, destroying a frigate, the forty-four-gun *Columbia*, and a sloop, the *Argus*. The British finished the job of burning what remained of the yard when they arrived. The British were also able to carry off two hundred American cannons, five hundred barrels of gunpowder and a hundred thousand musket cartridges. Although the Americans had burned and looted private buildings in Toronto, the British refrained from taking a full measure of revenge and, for the most part, destroyed public buildings only.

One exception was the house of Albert Gallatin, one of the American negotiators then meeting with the British in Ghent, which is in modern-day Belgium but was then a part of Holland. Snipers in the Gallatin house fired on the British when they came into range and the horse carrying General Ross was shot dead from under him. The snipers were cleared and the Gallatin house set on fire. Another private building set on fire was the office of a local newspaper, *The National Intelligencer*. Admiral Cockburn favored burning the entire city, on the theory that this would have forced the Americans to relocate their capital to New York City, where there was much Federalist opposition to the war that might influence national opinion; but General Ross did not let this happen. There was some looting, not by the British but by some of the Americans who had stayed in Washington while most of the residents fled. The leaders of Georgetown and Alexandria asked the British to spare their towns, and no damage was inflicted on Georgetown, though a naval force did attack Alexandria.

A nineteenth-century poet, Philip Freneau, evidently unaware or uncaring of the American attacks on Canadian towns, lamented the British attack on Washington this way:

A veteran host, by veterans led,
With Ross and Cockburn at their head,
They came — they saw — they burned — and fled!

They left our Congress naked walls —
Farewell to towers and capitols!
To lofty roofs and splendid halls!

To conquer armies in the field
Was, once, the surest method held
To make a battle country yield.

The warfare now the invaders make
Must surely keep us all awake,
Or life is lost for freedom's sake.

Margaret Bayard Smith, who established *The National Intelligencer* with her husband, Samuel Harrison Smith, and was a prolific writer for it, left a vivid account of the British attack on Washington in letters to her family. The invading British soldiers, she wrote, "never halted one moment, but marched in a solid mass — disregarding the dead bodies before them." She lamented that "our city was taken, the bridges and public buildings burnt, our troops flying in every direction." She reported seeing many dead horses in Washington and "nothing but blackened walls remained" at what had been the once majestic government buildings and offices. "We looked at the public buildings," Mrs. Smith wrote, "but none were so thoroughly destroyed as the President's House. Those beautiful pillars in the Representatives Hall were crack'd and broken. The roof, that noble dome, painted and carved with such beauty and skill, lay in ashes in the cellars beneath smoldering ruins, yet smoking." The Smiths visited the Madisons and Mrs. Smith reported, "Mrs. M. seem'd much depressed, she could scarcely speak without tears."

In trying to decide whether to attack first at Baltimore or Washington, or even Philadelphia, Admiral Cockburn argued that "Washington might be possessed without difficulty or opposition of any kind." The capture of a nation's capital was desirable, he said, because it was "always so great a blow to the government of a country, as well on account of the resources as of the documents and records the invading army is almost sure to obtain." Cockburn was correct about the ease of capturing Washington, and the rest of the world was amazed by the speed with which the British took and burned the capital of its enemy. General Ross said, "I trust all our differences with the Yankees will be shortly settled. That wish is I believe very prevalent among them, they feel strongly the disgrace of having lost their capital, taken by a handful of men, and blame very generally a government which went to war without the means or the abilities to carry it on. . . . The injury sustained by the city of Washington in the destruction of its public buildings has been immense and must disgust the country with a government that has left the capital unprotected."

A contemporary French military writer, Baron Henri de Jomini, whose works include a treatise on the art of war, wrote, "To the great astonishment of the world, a handful of seven or eight thousand English were seen to land in the middle of a state of ten million inhabitants, and penetrate far enough to get possession of the capital, and destroy all the public buildings; results for a parallel we should search history in vain. One would be tempted to set it down to the republican and unmilitary spirit of those states, if we had not seen the militia of Greece, Rome, and Switzerland make a better defense of their homes against far more powerful attacks."

Colonel Arthur Brooke, a British officer who kept a diary throughout the American campaign, wrote that the invaders burned "the Senate house (supposed to be one of the finest buildings in the world)." He went on. "The President's house, in which was found every thing ready for Dinner, table laid, Wine in, etc., etc., etc. I think this was one of the finest, and, at the same time, the most awful sights I ever witnessed—the Columns of fire issuing from the houses, and the Dock yard, the explosions of Magazines at intervals, the sky illuminated from the blazes." Brooke was amazed at the lack of opposition. "Next morning retired a little from the Town," he wrote, "as we could scarce think the Americans (from their immense population, and a well trained Artillery) would tamely allow a handful of British Soldiers, to advance thro' the heart of their Country, and burn, & destroy, the Capitol of the United States."

Secretary of War John Armstrong, who had insisted that the British would not attack Washington, resigned,

REMAINS OF THE CAPITOL AFTER THE FIRE.

The Capitol after the British burned it.

but the episode had little strategic importance. The humiliation suffered by the United States did, however, set into motion a unity, a sense of nationhood, that was to be raised further in the next attack by the British, the attempt to capture Baltimore. Secretary of State James Monroe wrote to Admiral Cochran, "In the course of ten years past the capitals of the principal powers of Europe have been conquered and occupied alternately by the victorious armies of each other; and no instance of such wanton and unjustifiable destruction has been seen."

Years later Theodore Roosevelt wrote harshly of President Madison and his government.

Some five thousand troops—regulars, sailors, and marines—were landed, under the command of General Ross. So utterly helpless was the Democratic Administration at Washington, that during the two years of warfare hardly any steps had been taken to protect the Capitol, or the country round about; what little was done, was done entirely too late, and bungled badly in addition. History has not yet done justice to the ludicrous and painful folly and stupidity of which the government founded by Jefferson, and carried on by Madison, was guilty, both in its preparations for, and in its way of carrying on, this war; nor is it yet realized that the men just mentioned, and their associates, are primarily responsible for the loss we suffered in it, and the bitter humiliation some of the incidents caused us. The small British army marched at will through Virginia and Maryland, burned Washington, and finally retreated from before Baltimore and re-embarked to take part in the expedition against New Orleans. Twice, at Bladensburg and North Point, it came in contact with superior numbers of militia in fairly good position. In each case the result was the same. After some preliminary skirmishing, maneuvering, and volley firing, the British charged with the bayonet. The rawest regiments among the American militia then broke at once; the others kept pretty steady, pouring in quite a destructive fire, until the regulars had come up close to them, when they also fled. The British regulars were too heavily loaded to pursue, and, owing to their mode of attack, and the rapidity with which their opponents ran away, the loss of the latter was in each case very slight. At North Point, however, the militia, being more experienced, behaved better than at Bladensburg. In neither case were the British put to any trouble to win their victory.

The above is a brief sketch of the campaigns of the war. It is not cheerful reading for an American.

Much of the credit for the victory in Washington was given to General Ross, a man of many talents and great ability. He was a dashing, courageous and possibly foolhardy soldier who was destined, one might have said, for a hero's death. He was born in Dublin in 1766, a product of the English establishment that ruled Ireland. He was an educated, cultured man who spoke French and Spanish fluently and was an accomplished violinist. He served in several army units, including the 20th Regiment, which he joined as it was being sent to Holland as part of a British-Russian army fighting Napoleon, and it was there that he was wounded for the first time. He later served in Minorca, an island in the Mediterranean, Egypt and Malta, finally being given command of a battalion. In 1806, he participated in an invasion of Calabria in southern Italy, where he received a medal for his fighting against the French at Maida. His regiment fought the French next in Portugal and Spain, and he received his second medal in a rearguard action and later a battle at Corunna in northern Spain. The regiment was sent back to Spain to fight Napoleon's army again in 1812 and Ross was made a major general in 1813 when he won yet another medal for valor near Pamplona, where he had horses shot out from under him twice. The duke of Wellington, then approaching his final victory over Napoleon, commended Ross for the courageous example he was setting for his troops. On February 27, 1814, Ross was badly wounded in the head during a battle at Orthez, but brushed it aside as "the hit I got in the chops."

This was the kind of soldier the Americans faced in Washington, while peace talks were being held by the Americans and British in Ghent. Ross wrote to his wife, Elizabeth Catherine Ross, whom he called affectionately Ly, from the Azores before setting out for the United States. "Negotiations we understand are going on between our government and the Yankees, so that my Ly must look to the prospect of our speeding meeting with glee and cheerfulness."

Twenty-four hours after he arrived in Washington, General Ross marched his troops back to the ships still at Benedict on the Patuxent, and the invaders set sail on September 10 to attack Baltimore, a much richer target than the provincial Washington. It is hard today to imagine the importance of Baltimore in 1814. Today it is an attractive, busy city, but not as important as it was then. In the 1810 census, Baltimore, with 46,555 residents, was the third-largest city in the United States, trailing only New York City (96,373) and Philadelphia (53,722). Baltimore had an excellent harbor that made it a center of shipping, shipbuilding, commerce and industry, and it had a strategic position at the head of the Patapsco River, which connected it to the Chesapeake Bay. Since the British had naval superiority in the Chesapeake, they would approach Baltimore by ship. And so the British headed toward Baltimore, where they would lose the battle and America would get its Star-Spangled Banner.

5

The Poet and the Flag Come Together

Before reaching Washington, the British had paused in Upper Marlboro, Maryland, where Major General Robert Ross and Rear Admiral George Cockburn set up their temporary headquarters on August 22, 1814, in Academy Hill, the finest residence in the town. It was the home of Dr. William Beanes, a physician who was about to play his role in the unfolding story of our flag and anthem. Beanes, who had little choice in the matter, supplied the British officers with wine and food, getting protection from destruction of his house in return. This was fine until the officers departed and Beanes was left in the same position as all the other Americans in the area, targets of the ordinary British soldiers looking for something to drink, something to eat and something to carry away as war booty. On August 28, as the British were withdrawing, some stragglers broke into Beanes's home and demanded food and drink, but instead were arrested by Beanes and his friends. One of the arrested stragglers escaped and made it back to the British lines, and General Ross sent back troops to arrest Beanes, who was taken aboard the flagship of the British force, the *Tonnant*.

Richard West, a patient of Dr. Beanes's, took a letter to General Ross from the governor of Maryland, Levin Winder, asking that Beanes, who was sixty-five years old, be freed, but Ross turned him down. Beanes faced trial for treason in Halifax, Nova Scotia, the British told West. The British were of the mistaken belief that Dr. Beanes was a recent immigrant from Scotland. In fact he was the third generation to have been born in America. Beanes had a tough time of it. When he was arrested, his captors made him sit on a mule facing the hind end. "With bare feet tied under the animal's belly," an early account said, "he was herded throughout the night and the next day to where the invading army was encamped. From there he was shipped as a brig prisoner on the flagship HMS *Tonnant* down the Chesapeake Bay." It got worse when he boarded the ship, where some of his captors threatened to hang him from the nearest yardarm.

West needed help from a lawyer in trying to free Beanes, so he went to Francis Scott Key in Georgetown. (Even though the ensuing events were pivotal in American history, history could not stand in the way of progress. Key's house was pulled down in 1947 to make way for approaches to the modern-day Key Bridge, which crosses the Potomac River between Washington and Arlington, Virginia.)

Key went to President James Madison and got permission to deal directly with General Ross. Without telling his wife, Polly, the nature of his mission lest she become apprehensive, he set off on September 3, accompanied by Colonel John S. Skinner, an American prisoner-of-war exchange officer, showing a flag of truce and carrying a letter, which argued that Beanes had been an unarmed civilian who should not have been arrested. On September 7 they arrived at General Ross's ship, the *Tonnant*, in the Chesapeake Bay. Skinner presented letters from wounded British soldiers who praised the American doctors who had treated them, persuading Ross to agree to Beanes's release for the good medical care, although it is not certain that Beanes was among those who treated the enemy soldiers. However, the British could not release Beanes, Key and Skinner while they were in the middle of planning the attack on Baltimore, lest the Americans tell their army what they knew of the plans. That reluctance to let Key leave the ship was another link in the chain of events leading to the composition of "The Star-Spangled Banner."

Another link was the decision made in 1813 by Major George Armistead to commission the making of a huge American flag to fly above Fort McHenry, which guarded the waters leading to Baltimore and was under his command. The order was given to Mary Pickersgill. Everything was now in place. If one element had been missing, we would not have "The Star-Spangled Banner" today as our national anthem. A soldier would successfully defend Baltimore and raise a huge flag that he had ordered, and the flag would be seen by a lawyer who had been brought to the scene on a mission of mercy, and it just so happened that the lawyer was a poet. If all these things had not happened, would we be singing "Yankee Doodle" as our national anthem? Probably not. "God Bless America"? Maybe. "Hail, Columbia"? Quite likely. "America the Beautiful"? Not a bad idea.

Mrs. Pickersgill's main helper was her thirteen-year-old daughter, Caroline—the only one of the four Pickersgill children to survive—and the two of them, plus some helpers, made the flag of four hundred yards of wool bunting. "No way she could have made that flag in six weeks on her own," said Sally Johnston, executive director of the Star-Spangled Banner Flag House in Baltimore, which was built in 1793. Also helping make the flag were three Pickersgill nieces, Margaret, Eliza and Jane Young. Mary Pickersgill's mother, Rebecca Young, was a flag maker and was living in the Pickersgill household at the time, so it is likely that she gave advice in making the Star-Spangled Banner, but Johnston doubts that she actually worked on it because she was very ill at the time and died in 1819. Both mother and daughter set up their flag businesses after being widowed, and "Mary grew up watching her mother make flags," Johnston said during a tour of the flag house. Flags were important for communications between ships in those days before radio, and a flag maker in a big port like Philadelphia or Baltimore could expect to make a good living. Mary Pickersgill was widowed in 1805 while living in Philadelphia and set up her business in Baltimore in 1807. "The fact that she immediately went into business when she came here shows that she was not wealthy," Johnston said.

The 1810 census shows that there were then nine people living in the Pickersgill house, eight women and a man. The man was probably a boarder, perhaps a sea captain who used his room when in port. Of the others, three may have been the nieces and two were black—a slave owned by Pickersgill and a free black woman who worked as a servant. Johnston said that the experts at the Flag House assumed that the slave and the free black woman both participated in the sewing, since Pickersgill needed the help of anyone she could get to finish the flag on time. Here is another case in which an otherwise admirable person turns out to have owned slaves. In fact, when Pickersgill died in 1857, she willed three slaves to her daughter. The matter of American patriots having owned slaves was usually ignored or glossed over in the past, and only now are people like those running historic sites addressing it directly.

The Flag House, a splendid little museum, was Mary Pickersgill's home and is where much of the Star-Spangled Banner was sewn. It has chunks of the flag that were removed as souvenirs over the years, antiques and furniture of the period, a painting by the nation's preeminent portraitist of that day, Charles Willson Peale (of her uncle, Colonel Benjamin Flower), and many other attractions.

The charity that Pickersgill once headed, the Impartial Female Humane Society, was established in 1802, making it the second-oldest retirement community in the United States. Only the Kearsley Retirement Community in Philadelphia, founded in 1772, is older. Its name was changed first to the Humane Impartial Society for Poor and Needy Needle Women, then to the Aged Women's and Aged Men's Home and later to the Pickersgill Retirement Community. It was moved in 1959 from downtown Baltimore to its present pleasant location on sixteen wooded acres in Towson, Maryland, a close-in suburb. The nonprofit community has ninety independent-living apartments, one hundred nine assisted-living units and sixty private rooms for people needing nursing care. It is a fine living memorial to the woman who made the Star-Spangled Banner.

Johnston has a notion as to what motivated Pickersgill to engage in good works like the shelter for poor women. "She saw her mother as a widow and saw all of her troubles and travails, and then became widowed herself," Johnston said. Her daughter, Caroline, was also widowed young, and she fell on hard times. "Caroline died in 1881 in the aged widows' home that her mother founded," Johnston said. "Mary never dreamed that's where she would end up." Indeed, Caroline once wrote, "I am widowed and childless, and now find myself, in my seventy-sixth year, in feeble health and with the barest pittance of support."

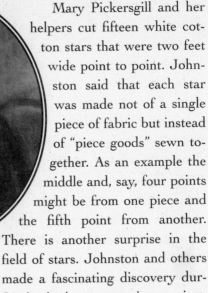

Mary Pickersgill

Mary Pickersgill and her helpers cut fifteen white cotton stars that were two feet wide point to point. Johnston said that each star was made not of a single piece of fabric but instead of "piece goods" sewn together. As an example the middle and, say, four points might be from one piece and the fifth point from another. There is another surprise in the field of stars. Johnston and others made a fascinating discovery during the Smithsonian Institution's conservation project, which began in 1999: The same stars are seen from both sides. Pickersgill first sewed on the stars on one side, then turned the flag over, cut out the part of the blue field under the stars, and then sewed down the stars to the blue field on the second side. This is known as the reverse appliqué method. "That was fun to find out," Johnston said. Since one side of the flag had been covered with canvas from 1873 until 1914, when the canvas was replaced with linen, this discovery could not be made until the backing was cut away, although there must have been a period in 1914 between the removal of the canvas and the addition of the linen backings when someone might have noticed it. Johnston estimates that 350,000 stitches were used to

The sewing of the Star-Spangled Banner.

sew the flag together. That's 350,000 individual stitches, *hand-sewn*, one by one. The eight red and seven white stripes are also two feet wide, but close inspection shows that, like the stars, the stripes are not made of single pieces. Instead, the stripes are pieced together with lengths of varying widths of bunting. The flag has fifteen stars and fifteen stripes, although there were eighteen states in the union by then. Yes, that's right—fifteen stripes. After the first flag of thirteen stars and stripes for the original colonies, two more stars and stripes had been added when Vermont became the fourteenth state in 1791 and Kentucky the fifteenth in 1792. Congress passed a law halting

The Flag House

further additions in 1794. It was not until 1818 that another law was passed requiring a star for each new state, then adding stars to the flag for Tennessee, number sixteen, admitted in 1796; Ohio, number seventeen, in 1803; and Louisiana, number eighteen, in 1812. Congress also recognized the frightful prospect of skinny red and white pinstripes by mandating that the flag should henceforth revert back to thirteen broad stripes, for the original thirteen states, adding a star for each new state but not a new stripe.

Mrs. Pickersgill may have bought the fabric for the flag from her brother-in-law, Captain Jesse Fearson, who owned a dry-goods store in Baltimore. The Pickersgills started work on the flag in their house and then, when it got too big, laid out the material on the floor of the malt-house of Claggett's Brewery, which was near the Pickersgill house. Claggett's is long since gone, but a new microbrewery was recently built there. They sewed the flag together, and when they were finished it was thirty feet, or three stories high, forty-two feet long, and weighed eighty pounds. That is relatively light when the size of 1,260 square feet is taken into account, but it had to be light in order to flap in the wind.

To get an idea of the size of the flag, consider that each star is twice as large as an adult's head and that, in its normal horizontal display of thirty feet high, that is the equivalent of five men six feet tall stacked one atop the other. The flag was made to fly from a ninety-foot flagpole, so it had to be big. It took Mrs. Pickersgill and her workers six weeks to make the flag in July and August 1813, and Mrs. Pickersgill turned it over to Armistead on August 19. On October 27, she was paid $405.90 for it, which is about $3,400 in today's money. Exact comparisons are not possible since wool is no longer used to make flags, but a flag of that size would cost about $2,000 today just for the cotton, which costs less than wool, according to an estimate from the National Flag & Display Company of Alexandria, Virginia. The equivalent cost of $3,400 is a fair price for that time because the War of 1812 had restricted trade, hurting the economy and causing great inflation in the United States.

Suzanne Thomassen-Krauss, a textile expert at the Smithsonian Institution, said of Mrs. Pickersgill, "She's an interesting lady, and her mother made a flag for George Washington's headquarters in Cambridge, Massachusetts." Thomassen-Krauss agreed with Johnston that the mother, Rebecca Young, probably gave advice to Mrs. Pickersgill on making the huge flag. Rebecca Young's maiden name was Flower, and her brother, Colonel Benjamin Flower, was a friend of Washington's and was in charge of buying military stores, and that may have helped her get the commission to make the flag for Washington. One of Colonel Flower's contributions to the Revolutionary War effort was saving the Liberty Bell from the invading British by taking it from Philadelphia to Lancaster, Pennsylvania. The British probably would have made it into cannon-balls. Family connections may also have contributed to Mary Pickersgill's contract for the Star-Spangled Banner. The order for the flag was given by Major Armistead, Commodore Joshua Barney and Brigadier General John S. Stricker. Pickersgill was related by marriage to both Barney and Stricker. This is not to suggest that Pickersgill was not qualified for the job. She, her mother and even her brother, William Young, were all noted flag makers in Philadelphia and Baltimore. The fact remains that years later Caroline Pickersgill wrote a letter to Major Armistead's daughter, Georgiana Armistead Appleton, in which she used the term *family connections* in parentheses when describing the Pickersgill selection for the job by Barney and Stricker.

The cotton for the stars was probably from the United States, but ironically, the wool most likely originated in

England, then the world's wool center. Thomassen-Krauss speculated that the wool might have been seized from a British ship by an American privateer or was bought in a third country after being shipped there from England. "Wool was the typical material for flags in this country up until the Civil War," Thomassen-Krauss said. "Cotton at that time—before the invention of the cotton gin—was a luxury item. Wool is good for a flag, being elastic and durable under wear and tear."

The blue dye for the star field in the Pickersgill flag was made of indigo, probably from India or Southeast Asia. The dye for the red stripes was made of cochineal, which comes from the dried bodies of female insects of the same name found in Mexico and the American Southwest, and madder, or *Rubia tinctorum*, from a plant probably grown in the Netherlands or France. The term *bunting*, describing the kind of wool used to make the flag, refers to an open-weave fabric. For the flag, the warp—the yarn stretched on the loom during weaving—and the weft—the filling yarn that is woven into the warp—are roughly thirty threads per inch for the blue field and forty-one for the stripes. The making of the Baltimore flag is thoroughly documented, but its construction is not nearly as well fixed in the public mind as the tale of Betsy Ross making the very first American flag in Philadelphia. I remember visiting the Betsy Ross House in Philadelphia as a boy and being told that this was where that first flag was made. The story of the making of the Baltimore flag has the advantage of being true, provable by accounts of the day and even the preservation of the bill of sale. The Betsy Ross story, on the other hand, is now believed by historians to have been concocted—or at least greatly elaborated on by her descendants. A bridge across the Delaware River connecting Philadelphia and southern New Jersey is named after Betsy Ross, testimony to the effectiveness of telling a fanciful story over and over. The official history of the flag by the Daughters of the American Revolution, which ought to know about these things, says that, because records are faulty, "it is difficult to confirm many of the claims as to the flag's original designer, maker or displayer. Soon after the flag was adopted, Congressman Francis Hopkinson claimed he had designed the flag and asked Congress for reimbursement. Since he was a public servant he was not paid." Betsy Ross, the DAR says, "was paid for making flags for the government as early as May 1777," or sometime after the first one is known to have been made.

When new, the Pickersgill flag was not fastened to its pole by grommets, since those metal eyelets did not come into use until later in the nineteenth century. Instead, there was a canvas sleeve, which has since been lost, that was attached to the side of the flag. A rope was run through the sleeve and stitched to it and the rope was then run up the pole.

After the burning of Washington, the head of the British force in North America, Vice Admiral Sir Alexander Cochrane, who had the authority to choose his targets, set sail for Baltimore, although the British high command in London thought he was going to attack New England. The earl of Liverpool wrote to the duke of Wellington, "They intend, on account of the season, to proceed in the first instance to the northward, and to occupy Rhode Island, where they propose living upon the country until about the 1st of November." That notion of living off the country in Rhode Island was not so farfetched. New England was the center of antiwar sentiment in the United States and secret conventions were held there to debate secession. After staying for a while in Rhode Island, Liverpool wrote, "They will then proceed again southward, destroy Baltimore, if they should find it practicable without too much risk, occupy several important points on the coast of Georgia and of the Carolinas, take possession of Mobile in the Floridas and close the campaign with an attack upon New Orleans."

The residents of Baltimore knew what to expect if the British could reach their city, since they had received word of the burning of Washington and, in fact, could see the flames of the burning capital thirty-five miles away. A suggestion of desperation appears in this notice published by a committee formed to defend the city: "Elderly men who are able to carry a firelock, and willing to render a last service to their country & posterity; are requested to meet at the Court House at 11 o'clock tomorrow, to form a company and be prepared to march in conjunction with the troops expected to move against the enemy." As the British prepared to attack Baltimore, Key, Skinner and

Beanes were transferred from the *Tonnant* to another warship, the *Surprise*, and then to the sloop that had brought Key and Skinner to the British fleet. This sloop, a craft known as a cartel, or truce boat, was now tethered to a British ship about eight miles below Fort McHenry. A number of British marines remained on Key's boat to make sure that no escape would be attempted.

On September 13, 1814, at seven o'clock in the morning, the British bombardment of Baltimore began. This was no Washington. This was a major American city, defended by Fort McHenry in the harbor and a force of 15,300 soldiers on land under the command of Major General Samuel Smith, who deployed them to meet the expected land attack to the east of the city. A song of the day warned:

> *The gen'ral gave orders for the troops to march down,*
> *To meet the proud Ross, and to check his ambition;*
> *To inform him we have decreed in our town*
> *That here he can't enter without permission.*
> *And if life he regards, he will not press too hard,*
> *For Baltimore freemen are ever prepared*
> *To check the presumptuous, whoever they be,*
> *That may rashly attempt to evade our decree.*

The British bombardment included fifteen hundred bombshells fired from the ships at Fort McHenry, but the large naval guns of the fort's battery kept the enemy from moving in close. To less effect, the Americans had sunk twenty-two or twenty-four ships in the river, according to differing accounts. The bombshells were designed to detonate as they neared their targets, the "bombs bursting in air," as Key was to write soon after the battle. Key's "rockets' red glare" comes from the British use of the Congreve rocket, which was invented in 1804 by Sir William Congreve, a British artillery officer, but it has its roots in thirteenth-century China. Congreve was inspired by fireworks, and today's Fourth of July rockets are similar to Congreve's. A Congreve rocket had a long stick attached to it. The stick was placed in a pipe held upright by a frame; the rocket was ignited and it burst out of the pipe. It was basically a big and deadly bottle rocket. The rockets used at Baltimore were four inches wide and forty-two inches long, and their fuses' length determined the height at which they would explode. The rockets were not very accurate but could be fired in a devastating barrage. Thirteen-inch mortar shells fired from cannons added more devastation to the "bombs bursting in air."

With the rain, and the smoke from the bombardment, Key and his American friends had no way of knowing how the battle was going. It was not until he saw the American flag still flying above Fort McHenry in the morning that he realized the British had failed to take the fort. In a letter sometime later to his best friend, John Randolph, a member of Congress from Virginia, Key described what he saw during the attack on Baltimore, providing further evidence that he opposed the war but, oddly, never mentioning that he had written "The Star-Spangled Banner" because of the bombardment he had witnessed.

You will be surprised to hear that I have spent eleven days in the British fleet. I went with a flag to endeavor to save poor old Dr. Beanes a voyage to Halifax, in which we fortunately succeeded. They detained us until after their attack on Baltimore, and you may imagine what a state of anxiety I endured. Sometimes when I remembered it was there that the declaration of this abominable war was received with public rejoicings, I could not feel a hope that they would escape; and again when I thought of the many faithful whose piety lessens that lump of wickedness I could hardly feel a fear.

To make my feelings still more acute, the Admiral intimated his fears that the town must be burned, and I was sure that if taken it would have been given up to plunder. I have reason to believe that such a promise was given to their soldiers. It was filled with women and children. I hope I shall never cease to feel the warmest gratitude when I think of this most merciful deliverance. It seems to have given me a higher idea of the "forbearance, long suffering and tender mercy" of God, than I had ever before conceived.

Never was a man more disappointed in his expectations than I have been as to the character of

British officers. With some exceptions they appeared to be illiberal, ignorant and vulgar, and seem filled with a spirit of malignity against everything American. Perhaps, however, I saw them in unfavorable circumstances.

Key next describes a British attempt to slip past Fort McHenry in a flanking movement that ultimately failed, his language filled with the terror of the night, his avocation of poet easy to comprehend.

Between two and three o'clock in the morning the British, with one or two rocket and several bomb-vessels manned by 1,200 picked men, attempted, under cover of darkness, to slip past the fort and up to Patapsco, hoping to effect a landing and attack the garrison at the rear.

Succeeding in evading the guns of the fort, but unmindful for Fort Covington, under whose batteries they came, their enthusiasm over the supposed success of the venture gave way in a derisive cheer, which, borne by the damp night air to our small party of Americans on the *Minden*, must have chilled the blood in their veins and pierced their patriotic hearts like a dagger.

The *Minden* is thought by some to have been the name of Key's truce boat, but other experts disagree and the name is not known with certainty. Lonn Taylor, a historian at

the National Museum of American History at the Smithsonian Institution and an authority on the flag, writes that
the boat was probably called the *President*.

Key continued:

Fort Covington, the *lazaretto* [a hospital for people with contagious diseases, derived from Lazarus,
the diseased beggar from the Bible. Baltimore's *lazaretto* was put to military use during the War of 1812],
and the American barges in the river now simultaneously poured a galling fire upon the unprotected
enemy, raking them fore and aft, in horrible slaugh-
ter. Disappointed and disheartened, many wounded
and dying, they endeavored to regain their ships,
which came closer to the fortifications in an endeavor to protect the retreat. A fierce battle ensued.
Fort McHenry opened the full force of all her batteries upon them as they repassed, and the fleet re-
sponding with entire broadsides made an explosion
so terrific that it seemed as though mother earth
had opened and was vomiting shot and shell in a
sheet of fire and brimstone.

The heavens aglow were a seething sea of flame,
and the waters of the harbor, lashed into an angry
sea by vibrations, the *Minden* rode and tossed as
though in a tempest. It is recorded that the houses
in the city of Baltimore, two miles distant, were
shaken to their foundations. Above the tempes-

tuous roar, intermingled with its hubbub and confusion, were heard the shrieks and groans of the dying and wounded. But alas! they were from the direction of the fort. What did it mean? For over an hour the pandemonium reigned. Suddenly it ceased—all was quiet, not a shot fired or sound heard, a deathlike stillness prevailed, as the darkness of night resumed its sway. The awful stillness and suspense were unbearable.

Armistead gave this official account of the attempted British flanking attack:

The enemy continued throwing shells, with one or two slight intermissions, till 1 o'clock on the morning of Wednesday, when it was discovered that he had availed himself of the darkness of the night, and had thrown a considerable force above to our right; they had approached very near to Fort Covington, when they began to throw rockets, intended, I presume, to give them an opportunity of examining the shores—as I have since understood, they had detached 1,250 picked men, with scaling ladders, for the purpose of storming this fort. We once more had an opportunity of opening our batteries, and kept up a continued blaze for nearly two hours, which had the effect again to drive them off.

Key waited for the dawn. "At last it came. A bright streak of gold mingled with crimson shot athwart the eastern sky, followed by another and still another, as the morning sun rose in the fullness of his glory, lifting 'the mists of the deep,' crowning a 'Heaven-blest land' with a new victory and grandeur." There was not yet a national anthem, so when it became clear that Fort McHenry had withstood the British attack, the huge Star-Spangled Banner was run up the flagpole to the tune of "Yankee Doodle."

Contrary to popular belief, that flag is not the one that flew over Fort McHenry during the British bombardment. It was raining then and forts did not fly their prized flags in the rain, especially a woolen one that would shrink. Instead, the flag flying at Fort McHenry that night was a smaller and less valuable banner called a storm flag. The storm flag was also made by the Pickersgills and it was twenty-five by seventeen feet, a more normal size, about a third as large as what has come to be known as the Star-Spangled Banner. Pickersgill was paid $168.54 for the storm flag, about $1,404 in today's money. By dawn's early light, if we may borrow a bit of the poetry here, the rain had stopped and Armistead had the huge Pickersgill flag run up, and that is what Key then saw. That version is supported by an eyewitness account from a young British naval officer, Robert J. Barrett, who wrote that, as the British sailed away, the Americans "hoisted a most superb and splendid ensign on their battery." There has been some speculation that the opening phrase, "O say can you see" (some versions, including the first printing, have an exclamation mark after the *O* and grammar would seem to require some punctuation after *say*, but Key's manuscript has neither), was inspired by a question from the good Dr. Beanes, who was a bit nearsighted and could not see that far himself. Maybe it happened that way, but the tale does seem a bit contrived.

There is an old legend in American history that Abe Lincoln scribbled the Gettysburg Address on the back of an envelope. This is not true. But is this the source of the legend? Key began to write "The Star-Spangled Banner" on the back of a letter that he had in his pocket. After the British left, Key wrote more during the trip to Baltimore and wrote the rest of it in the Indian Queen Hotel.

The original version of the poem by Key is owned by the Maryland Historical Society in Baltimore and the Library of Congress has the only other copy in Key's hand that is known to exist. Key is known to have made just five copies and the whereabouts of the other three are unknown. Key made slight variations in each, so it might be argued that there is not a truly authentic version of his poem.

Key's brother-in-law, Judge Joseph H. Nicholson, the second-in-command at Fort McHenry, was very much taken by Key's poem and brought it to a local printing shop owned by Captain Benjamin Edes at Baltimore and Gay Streets, where Edes's apprentice, Samuels Sands, set it in type and printed copies of it in handbill form. The copies were circulated around Baltimore under the title

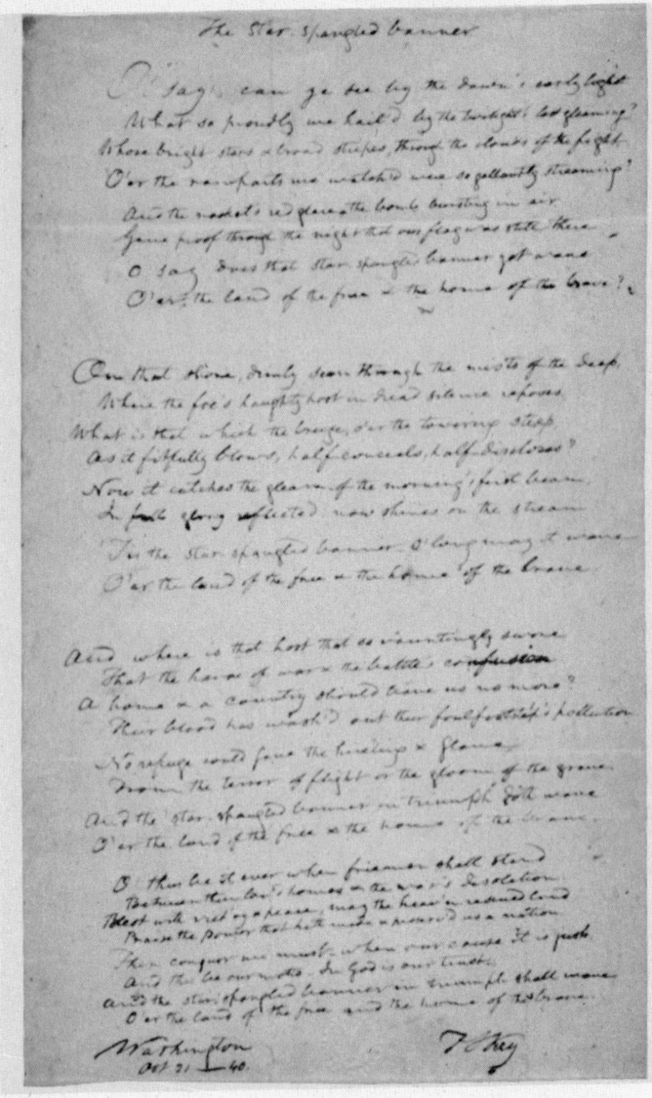

Francis Scott Key's manuscript of the Star-Spangled Banner.

"The Defence of Fort McHenry," a name evidently given to it by Nicholson. Others suggest that Key's companion, Skinner, was the one who got the copies printed. Note that Americans were still using the British spelling for *defence*.

A descendant of Key's, Francis Key-Smith, took up the story in a biography of Key that he wrote.

Copies of the song were struck off in handbill form, and promiscuously distributed on the street. Catching with popular favor like prairie fire it spread in every direction, was read and discussed, until, in less than an hour, the news was all over the city.

Picked up by a crowd of soldiers assembled, some accounts put it, about Captain McCauley's tavern, next to the Holiday Street Theater, others have it around their tents on the outskirts of the city, Ferdinand Durang, a musician, adapted the words to the old tune of "Anacreon in Heaven," and, mounting a chair, rendered it in fine style.

On the evening of the same day it was again rendered upon the stage of the Holiday Street Theater by an actress, and the theater is said to have gained thereby a national reputation. In about a fortnight it had reached New Orleans and was publicly played by a military band, and shortly thereafter was heard in nearly, if not all, the principal cities and towns throughout the country.

On September 20, 1814, "The Star-Spangled Banner," by then given its new name by Key, was published as a poem in *The Baltimore Patriot* and then reprinted by other newspapers around the country. At some point, the notation "Tune: Anacreon in Heaven" was added, and in October the poem was sung to that tune in Baltimore by actor Charles Durang, Ferdinand's brother. Only ten copies of the original printed version with the music, entitled "The Star Spangled Banner: A Patriotic Song" (note the absence of the hyphen in *Star Spangled*), are known to exist, and the Library of Congress has one. It is marked "Baltimore, Printed and Sold at CARRS Music Store 56 Baltimore Street. The original printed version carries a time signature of 6/4—six beats to a measure, with a quarternote getting one beat—as opposed to the 3/4 time used today. The original song, also known as "The Anacreontic Song," is about a Greek poet who lived from 572 to 488 B.C., dates that are approximate and are given differently by various authorities. Anacreon was born in Teos, in what is now Turkey, and later lived in Athens. He wrote satires and love poems, most of which are lost.

"To Anacreon in Heaven" was an English drinking song that was enormously popular in both Britain and the United States, so it is quite understandable that Key had the tune in his head and that people adopted Key's words quickly. Taverns were the main everyday gathering place in those days, which accounts for the popularity of a drinking song. The original music has obscure origins, but it may have been written by a London composer and musician, John Stafford Smith (1750–1836). "Anacreon in Heaven" was first performed in Baltimore earlier in 1814 and had become so popular that people wrote many parodies on it, according to Wayne Shirley, a music expert at the Library of Congress. Key probably had one of those derivatives in his head as he composed the poem, because his words fit the rhythm of the music of "Anacreon" exactly, and he had used it before in composing a poem in honor of Stephen Decatur, the American naval hero.

Here are the words of "The Anacreontic Song," written by Ralph Tomlinson, a onetime president of the Anacreontic Society.

> *To Anacreon in Heav'n, where he sat in full glee,*
> *A few Sons of Harmony sent a petition;*
> *That he their Inspirer and Patron wou'd be;*
> *When this answer arrived from the Jolly Old Grecian;*
> *"Voice, Fiddle, and Flute,*
> *No longer be mute,*
> *I'll lend you my name and inspire you to boot,*
> *And besides I'll instruct you like me, to intwine,*
> *The Myrtle of Venus with Bacchus's Vine."*

I guess you had to be there.

The use of "Anacreon" came with a price. Americans have struggled to sing "The Star-Spangled Banner" ever since because its range is outside most people's abilities. "The Star-Spangled Banner" increased in popularity steadily

Sheet music for Anacreon in Heaven.

over the years and finally was adopted as America's national anthem on March 3, 1931.

Francis Scott Key

Francis Scott Key was a lawyer and public official, and a part-time military officer in the War of 1812 despite his opposition to the war on religious grounds. He served in the Maryland militia as a lieutenant in the Georgetown Light Artillery, seeing combat at Bladensburg. And he was a poet of some ability; consider how long his work about Fort McHenry has endured. He did many things in his life, including arguing cases before the Supreme Court, but the composition of "The Star-Spangled Banner" was his crowning achievement, his singular moment of fame. Without it, no one would know his name today.

Key described the events of that day in a speech in Frederick, Maryland, years later.

I saw the flag of my country waving over a city, the strength and pride of my native state, a city devoted to plunder and desolation by its assailants. I witnessed the preparation for its assaults. I saw the array of its enemies as they advanced to the attack. I heard the sound of battle. The noise of the

Francis Scott Key portrait at St. John's Episcopal Church, Georgetown Parish

conflict fell upon my listening ear and told me that the brave and the free had met the invaders.

It could be said that the twenty-five hour ordeal Fort McHenry withstood under British guns on September 13 and 14, 1814, was the day we became a nation. Certainly the American nation, singing Key's song, found a greater devotion to the union, setting into motion a love of the flag as well, although that reverence did not reach its present level until the Civil War. America does not have the kings and queens of royalty, and there is not an officially sanctioned religion. It has the greatest democratic document ever written, the Constitution, and when the nation salutes the flag or sings Key's song, there is a strength greater than any throne or church. This was Key's shining moment, his one great good deed, something never to be repeated.

There is a portrait of Key in the assembly room of his old congregation, St. John's Episcopal Church in Georgetown. It hangs with no great attention called to it, too high on the wall to be noticed in passing. It is not very artful, but at least it gives us an idea of what he looked like. Key was an active member of St. John's Church, which he served as a lay minister. He had once considered a career in the church.

Another St. John's, St. John's College in Annapolis, Maryland, also was important to Key's life. He entered St. John's when he was ten years old and the college still a grammar school. He went through to the intermediate school and then took three years of college work, graduating at the age of seventeen in 1776 as valedictorian of his twelve-member class. During his days as a schoolboy, according to an official history of St. John's, "Key galloped a cow around the college green, devised tricks against unpopular teachers, 'ushers' they were called, according to a friend, was constantly 'getting into scrapes by writing pasquinades on odd characters in the town,' " the term *pasquinade* referring to a satire or lampoon. Thirty-one years after his graduation, Key led the effort to establish an alumni association at St. John's, which was threatened with closure when Maryland withdrew almost all of its state aid as an economy measure. He was successful and the college was saved, largely because of his efforts. Speaking at that first alumni meeting, on February 22, 1827, Key defined the roles of a college this way:

> It is to give strength and preparation for the whole life. It is then that habits, principles and tastes, that fix the color of succeeding years, are to be formed. Then are the victories to be achieved

over the temper and disposition, over the temptations from within, and from without, that make the man master of himself through life. Patience in investigation, accuracy of research, perseverance in labor, resolution to conquer difficulty, zeal in the cause of learning and virtue, are then to be acquired. Then is Science to display her charms, and Literature her delights, and a refined and exalted taste to lure him, by higher gratifications, from the vain pleasures of the world. Then is he to be made familiar with the sages and heroes of antiquity, to catch the inspiration of their genius and their virtue, and the great and the good of every age and of every land are to be made his associates, his instructors, his examples.

That is hardly the description of most American colleges today.

According to another history of St. John's, the school felt that graduates must perform some kind of public act to symbolize their entry into the company of educated men. Key certainly performed an everlasting public act the night that Fort McHenry was bombarded by the British. The eighteenth century was an age of great oratory, and this art was emphasized at St. John's. The college history described Key's speech at St. Anne's as "very elegant, very elevated, and very dull."

Regarding slavery, Key was somewhat ambivalent. He was an admirer of William Wilberforce, the English statesman and writer, and one of the great leaders of the antislavery movement in Britain. In 1816, Key, saying he hated slavery, helped to found the American Colonization Society, which had as its goal the transfer of American slaves and other blacks to Africa, a halfway measure that was opposed by both the slaveholders and the abolitionists. Implicit in such a goal was the notion that blacks would never be the equals of whites, that a black was a less worthy citizen than a white. It also was based on a failure to realize that most of the slaves of that day had been born in America and had never seen what the promoters of the plan regarded as their native land. The American Colonization Society partly succeeded in its goal. Although slavery continued until the Civil War ended it, the society established the West African nation of Liberia and colonized it with former American slaves. The capital was named Monrovia, after President James Monroe, Madison's successor and another of the slave-owning American presidents.

The American Colonization Society's membership was made up of prominent white men, many of them, like Key, slaveholders. Some were people who wanted to end slavery and some were racists who wanted free blacks to be settled in Africa while they continued to own slaves. Free blacks generally opposed the plan, choosing instead to remain in the United States and stay in the fight against slavery. As a result, only six thousand free blacks immigrated to Liberia between 1820 and 1850.

There are two more great ironies concerning Francis Scott Key's role in this tale. Despite the attention that Key drew to the flag with "The Star-Spangled Banner," no flag was displayed at his funeral in 1843. And despite the fame that he brought to Fort McHenry, Key never visited it.

6

A Hero's Death

The attack on Baltimore was both a land and sea operation. The bombardment of Fort McHenry is known to all Americans because of "The Star-Spangled Banner," but the second part, the land war, was equally important and is hardly remembered today. If the British had marched from Washington to Baltimore, they would have found an almost defenseless city, but they did not think they had the equipment to attack Baltimore by an overland approach. They wanted to take advantage of their naval power and move by ship. The British landed their army at North Point on the eastern shore of the Patapsco River, about fifteen miles south of Baltimore, on September 12. The Americans had deduced that the British would land there because it was the closest that the big British ships could

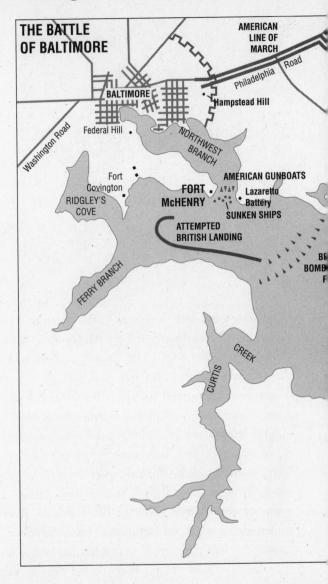

THE BATTLE
OF BALTIMORE

AMERICAN
LINE OF
MARCH

Philadelphia Road

BALTIMORE

Hampstead Hill

Washington Road

Federal Hill

NORTHWEST
BRANCH

Fort
Covington

RIDGLEY'S
COVE

AMERICAN GUNBOATS

FORT
McHENRY

Lazaretto
Battery

SUNKEN SHIPS

ATTEMPTED
BRITISH LANDING

BR
BOMB
F

FERRY BRANCH

CREEK

CURTIS

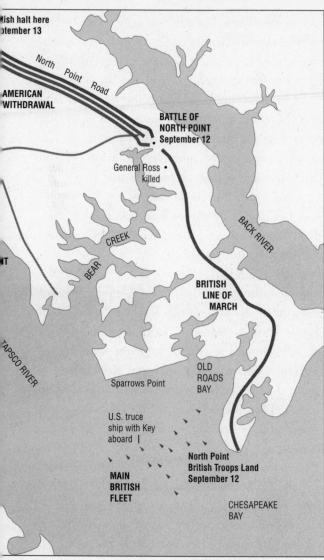

The Battle of Baltimore

approach on the east bank, since the channel was too shallow closer to the city to allow its use by large-draft vessels. The west bank was too marshy for a landing. An officer who served in the British expedition wrote, "It was determined to land here rather than ascend the river, because the Patapsco, though broad, is far from deep. It is, in fact, too shallow to admit a line-of-battle ship; and, as no one could guess what impediments might be thrown in the way to obstruct navigation, prudence forbade that five thousand men should be entrusted to the convoy of smaller vessels alone. Besides, the distance from this point to Baltimore did not exceed fourteen or fifteen miles; a space which might easily be traversed in a day."

So the invaders landed at North Point, and for the British, tragedy struck quickly. Major General Robert Ross—always on the front lines of his troops, the hero of the Napoleonic wars, a soldier who so often barely escaped death as his horses were shot out from under him— was shot dead by a sniper. In his usual way, Ross had gone up to the front during the first skirmish and was downed by a single shot. The official history of the 20th Regiment described Ross's death this way:

All the troops and marines, numbering about four thousand men, disembarked and marched towards Baltimore. The route lay through an impenetrably wooded country, and riflemen might be concealed in every thicket, invisible except to the eye of an Indian. General Ross and Admiral Cockburn were both with light troops in front of the column. At a sudden turning in the road a corps of enemy was observed, whose right was supported by a wood which lay on our left; into this wood the enemy's right extended. A fire was opened simultaneously upon our advance by these troops, and by half a dozen rifles in a copse to our right. It was there that the gallant Ross received his mortal wound; the ball passed through his right arm into his breast. The advancing soldiers knew their general had been struck down, as his horse, with an empty saddle, dashed past them a moment later, and they passed the dying hero, as he lay under a tree, his life blood welling away. He was carried to the boats at North Point, but expired before they were reached.

The last moments of this distinguished soldier are thus described by Admiral Cockburne in his dispatch to Vice-Admiral Hon. Sir Alexander Cochrane, dated HMS *Severn*, 15th September, 1814. They show what a noble, unselfish man he was; not a thought of his own pain and sufferings, but for all those whom he was leaving. "It is with the most heartfelt sorrow I have to add in this short and desultory skirmish my gallant and highly valued friend the Major-General received a musket ball through his arm into his breast, which proved fatal to him on his way to the waterside for embarkation. Our country, sir, has lost in him one of its best and bravest soldiers, and those who knew him, as I did, a friend most honored and beloved; and I trust, sir, I may be forgiven for considering it a sacred duty to mention here that whilst his wounds were binding up, and we were placing him on the bearer, which was to carry him off the field, he assured me the wounds he had received in the performance of his duty to his country caused him not a pang; but he felt anxiety for a wife and family dearer to him than his life, whom in the event of the fatal termination he foresaw, he recommended to the protection and notice of H. M. Government and the country.

The loss of General Ross was of immense importance to the battle for Baltimore. Another section of the regimental history quotes John Murray, an officer who was at the scene, as having said that it was impossible to determine the effect that Ross's death would have but that "a sort of involuntary groan ran from rank to rank" as word of it spread. Murray's description follows here after the official regimental account, which continued:

According to an officer who was present at Baltimore, "The death of General Ross, in short, seemed to have disorganized the whole plan of proceedings, and the fleet and army rested idle, like a watch without its mainspring." The body of the general was placed on board HMS *Tonnant*, and conveyed to Halifax, Nova Scotia, where it was accorded a public funeral on the 30th of September. A monument was raised to his memory by the officers of the garrison.

If General Ross's services in America can be measured by the rejoicings of the enemy over his death, they were indeed great. On the news being known the most enthusiastic exultations were manifested in Baltimore; at least a dozen men claimed the honor of having shot him, and the same number of rifles were exhibited as the identical weapon from which the fatal ball had been fired.

The following is from the letter written by John Murray, the officer in the invasion cited above:

We were now drawing near the scene of action, when another officer came at full speed towards us, with horror and dismay in his countenance; and calling aloud for a surgeon. Every man felt within himself that all was not right, though none was willing to believe the whispers of his own terror. But what at first we could not guess at, because we dreaded it so much, was soon realized; for the aide-de-camp had scarcely passed, when the general's horse, without its rider, and with the saddle and housings stained with blood, came plunging onwards. Nor was much time given for fearful surmise, as to the extent of our misfortune. In a few moments we reached the ground where the skirmishing had taken place, and beheld

Heroic sculpture of Maj. Gen. Robert Ross
in St. Paul's Cathedral, London.

poor Ross laid, by the side of the road, under a canopy of blankets, and apparently in the agonies of death. As soon as the firing began, he had ridden to the front, that he might ascertain from whence it originated, and, mingling with the skirmishers, was shot in the side by a rifleman. The wound was mortal: he fell into the arms of his aide-de-camp, and lived only long enough to name his wife, and to commend his family to the protection of his country. He was removed towards the fleet, but expired before his bearers could reach the boats.

It is impossible to conceive the effect which this melancholy spectacle produced throughout the army. By the courtesy and condescension of his manners, General Ross had secured the absolute love of all who served under him, from the highest to the lowest; and his success on a former occasion, as well as his judicious arrangements on the present, had inspired every one with the most perfect confidence in his abilities. His very error, if error it may be called, in so young a leader—I mean that diffidence in himself which had occasioned some loss of time on the march to Washington—appeared now to have left him. His movements were at once rapid and cautious; nay, his very countenance indicated a fixed determination, and a perfect security of success. All eyes were turned upon him as we passed, and a sort of involuntary groan ran from rank to rank, from the front to the rear of the column.

"These Americans are not to be trifled with," a British naval lieutenant, G. G. MacDonald, said when Ross was shot.

The impact of Ross's death reached the highest level in Britain. The Prince Regent—later King George IV but then serving from the throne in place of his deranged father, George III, whom we Americans will remember from the Revolution—praised Ross in an address read to Parliament on November 8, 1814, lamenting his loss and commanding that his family designation should henceforth be Ross of Bladensberg (a slight misspelling of Bladensburg). An addition was made to the Ross family's crest: a general's arm, with laurel wreath around it, issuing from a crown, grasping the broken flag of the United States. A monument to Ross was placed in St. Paul's Cathedral, London, of which the 20th Regiment's history says, "In the national monument, which is tabular, there is little to admire. Britannia is represented weeping over the tomb of the departed warrior, on which an American flag is being deposited by a nude figure of Valour, while Fame descends with a wreath of laurels to crown the hero's head." The Ross monument is a cenotaph, a memorial without the body. He was buried in Halifax, Nova Scotia, in Old St. Paul's Cemetery.

One American account suggested that the setback to the British by Ross's death was twofold—the unquestioned devastating effect on British morale as well as the loss of a great military leader. A British officer on the scene said that Ross's successor, Colonel Arthur Brooke, was "an officer of decided personal courage, but, perhaps, better calculated to lead a battalion than to guide an army."

Another British officer, Captain Edward Crofton, said of General Ross's death, "Thus fell at an early age one of the brightest ornaments of his profession, who, whether at the head of a regiment, a brigade, or a corps, had alike displayed the talents of command, who was not less beloved in his private than enthusiastically admired in his public character, and whose only fault, if it may be deemed so, was an excess of gallantry, enterprise and devotion to the service."

Crofton's account of what happened next suggests how much the British had lost with the death of Ross and his leadership. Crofton said that the British "pushed to within five miles of Baltimore, where a corps of about six thousand men, six pieces of artillery and some hundred cavalry were discovered posed under cover of a wood." The British attacked and, Crofton reported, "in less than fifteen minutes the enemy's force, being utterly broken and dispersed, fled in every direction over the country, leaving on the field two pieces of cannon with a considerable number of killed, wounded and prisoners. The enemy lost in the short but brilliant affair from five to six hundred in killed and wounded, while at the most moderate confrontation he is at least one thousand hors de combat."

To read Crofton's account, one would wonder why the British lost. Although he wrote that he had a superior army force, he was depending on the navy for support. The night before the planned attack, he wrote, "I received a communication from the Commander in Chief of the Naval Forces, by which I was informed, that in consequence of the entrance to the harbor being closed up by vessels sunk for that purpose by the enemy, a naval cooperation against the town and camp was found impracticable. Under these circumstances, and keeping in view your lordship's instructions, it was agreed between the Vice Admiral and myself that the capture of this town would not have been a sufficient equivalent to the loss which might probably be sustained in storming the heights." Crofton found consolation in the fact that the Americans had sunk twenty vessels or more to prevent the British from sailing closer to Baltimore. Crofton said the British withdrew from Baltimore and "reembarked the army at North Point not having a wounded man behind, and carrying with me about two hundred prisoners."

Ross was not the only British officer to die a hero's death. Before the attack on Baltimore, the British attacked several towns on the Chesapeake Bay. One was Moor-fields, near Chestertown, Maryland, which was the target of a force of naval and marine raiders from a British frigate, the *Menelaus*, led by Sir Peter Parker, described by one contemporary as "the handsomest man in the navy." Parker was at the head on the force in a fight with the Maryland militia when he was struck by a musket ball that cut the main artery in his thigh. "They have hit me, Pearce," he said to a subordinate officer, "but it is nothing! Push on, my brave boys, and follow me!" Parker bled to death before he could be returned to the *Menelaus* for treatment and his body, preserved in a barrel of spirits, probably rum, in the custom of the day, was conveyed first to Bermuda for a public funeral and then to England for another. A poetic eulogy was written about him by the poet Lord Byron, his cousin.

Before the British landing, Ross had boasted that he would make Baltimore his winter quarters, and its capture would have been a great setback for the Americans. The British wanted to take it because many of the swift priva-teers that preyed on British merchant shipping were built there and because it was a hotbed of prowar sentiment. "It is a doomed town," one British naval officer declared as the attack was planned. The extent of the prowar sentiment could be seen in public demonstrations in 1812 against an antiwar newspaper in Baltimore, *The Federal Republican*. The newspaper supported the business interests that were being harmed by shipping restrictions associated with the war. The editor said, "We mean to represent, in as strong colors as we are capable, that the war is unnecessary, inexpedient, and entered into from partial, personal, and, as we believe, motives bearing upon their front marks of undisguised foreign influence which cannot be mistaken," the last reference being to the French.

Two days later, a mob descended upon the newspaper's office and destroyed it. The publisher resumed printing the paper five weeks later and the place was attacked again. In that raid, twenty people had taken up stations inside the newspaper office, and the mob broke in and started up the stairs. The defenders fired on the mob, killing one of the ringleaders and wounding several others. The militia was called out and the defenders were taken to jail to answer a murder charge, and at night a mob attacked the prison, forcing their way in. Some of the newspaper's defenders escaped by melting into the crowd, but several of them were brutally beaten, including General James McCubbin Lingan, a hero of the Revolution, who died from his beating. Lingan had survived a British prison ship during the Revolutionary War and was appointed collector of the port of Georgetown after independence, only to die at the hands of an American mob. The city magistrates conducted an investigation and concluded that the newspaper was to blame for the attacks. In time of war, they said, no one has the right to put obstructions in the path of the country's war effort.

Among the Federalist opponents of the War of 1812 was James McHenry, for whom the fort was named. He served for a time as secretary of war during the presidencies of George Washington and John Adams, living near Baltimore while the battle for the city was going on. The Federalist antiwar sentiment, concentrated in New England, was so strong that President James Madison wrote in 1812 to his predecessor, Thomas Jefferson, "The seditious opposition in Massachusetts and Connecticut, with intrigues elsewhere insidiously co-operating with it, have so clogged the wheels of the war that I feel the campaign will not accomplish the object of it."

Of course, the battle looked different to the American defenders. On the evening of September 11, 1814, a balmy Sunday evening lit by a bright moon shining from a cloudless sky, the British fleet arrived at the mouth of the Patapsco River, about two miles off North Point. This put the British about twelve miles from Baltimore by water and about fifteen by land. At about two o'clock on the morning of September 12, the British force started going ashore. One American account puts the invaders' strength twice as high as the British report of four thousand. On the other hand, Colonel Brooke put his British force at three thousand men facing twelve thousand Americans, an exaggeration that was cast in stone when the British raised the statue in Ross's memory with an inscription that says he was "killed while directing a successful attack upon a superior force." It seems that winners are prone to exaggerating the size of their enemy—it enhances their accomplishment—and losers are just as likely to understate the size of their own force—it suggests a cause of the defeat.

The British carried rations for three days, enough time, they calculated, to capture Baltimore. Ross had said he would eat his next Sunday dinner there. While accounts of the opposing armies' sizes varied greatly, there is no doubt that the British, who had just finished off Napoleon, were better trained than the Americans, who were largely part-time militiamen. Exaggerations even extended to casualty reports. In the fighting along the approach from North Point to Baltimore, Brooke reported that his troops had killed or wounded five hundred Americans and had taken a thousand prisoners. For the same period, the Americans reported the loss of twenty-four killed, one hundred thirty-nine wounded and fifty taken prisoner.

When American intelligence reported the British movement, Major General Samuel Smith, who was in command of the Baltimore defense, sent more than three thousand troops to meet the British. As the British land force moved toward Baltimore, its fleet moved upriver and prepared to attack Fort McHenry, which guarded the water approach to the city. General Ross and his navy counterpart, Rear Admiral George Cockburn, rode at the head of the British force for about an hour without encountering

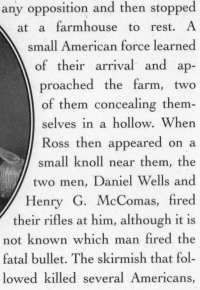

any opposition and then stopped at a farmhouse to rest. A small American force learned of their arrival and approached the farm, two of them concealing themselves in a hollow. When Ross then appeared on a small knoll near them, the two men, Daniel Wells and Henry G. McComas, fired their rifles at him, although it is not known which man fired the fatal bullet. The skirmish that followed killed several Americans, including Wells and McComas, two young men who had been saddlery apprentices. The official history of Ross's 20th Regiment identifies another American volunteer, Aquila Randall, as the soldier who fired the fatal shot.

General Samuel Smith

The Americans, far outnumbered, fell back, and the British land force advanced toward Baltimore. The next day, Tuesday, September 13, the British fleet reached a point two miles below Fort McHenry, a star-shaped installation with cannons installed on each of the points. Fort McHenry sits on Whetstone Point, guarding the approach to Baltimore on the Patapsco River, and cost almost forty thousand dollars when it was built in 1779. Since comparisons with the dollar before 1800 are inaccurate, this sum cannot be put into today's dollars. The fort

Fort McHenry

was designed by Jean Foncin, a French engineer. Fort McHenry was bombarded from six o'clock in the morning until seven o'clock in the morning of the next day, September 14. Major George Armistead, Fort McHenry's commander, ordered his gunners to return fire, but the British ships were outside of their range. Fort McHenry, however, was within the range of the British mortars, which fired fifteen hundred bombs and seven hundred rockets at it. Despite the great firepower, only four Americans defending Fort McHenry were killed—Lieutenant Levi Claggett and Sergeant John Clemm, both Baltimore merchants, and Charles Messinger and Thomas Beeston—and twenty-four were wounded.

It was here that the British overreached. Vice-Admiral

Sir Alexander Cochrane, who was in command of the British expedition, ordered three gunships to move closer to increase the chances of their damaging the fort, but this brought them within range of Fort McHenry's guns, and Major Armistead ordered that a cannonade be directed at them. The American response forced the three gunships to withdraw after half an hour and one of them, the *Erebus*, was so damaged that it had to be towed to safety. The two sides exchanged cannon fire into the night, during which a British force left the fleet by barge and attempted to capture nearby Fort Covington, which led the Fort McHenry gunners to turn their fire on them as well, helping to drive them off. It was this terrific exchange of cannon—the noise, the flashes of explosions—that Francis Scott Key witnessed.

As the river stalemate continued, the British land force moved toward Baltimore and General Smith then concentrated his defenders in its path. The British, their strength depleted by battle, now calculated that they were far outnumbered by the Americans. Because of the guns of Fort McHenry and because of the obstruction from sunken boats in the river, the British army was deprived of covering fire from the ships on the river. When a small flanking naval attack was repulsed, the British hopes for capturing Baltimore vanished.

Despite all of the heroics, most Americans know little about the War of 1812. Scott S. Sheads, a ranger at Fort McHenry and a prolific writer who has studied the fighting in the Chesapeake area, has written that "Bladens-

burg, perhaps one of the dark-
est defeats in American history, is remembered only
for the British burning
of the White House and
Dolley Madison's sav-
ing of Gilbert Stuart's
portrait of Washington
and the Declaration of
Independence, stuffed
in a wagon during the
frantic American retreat."
He says that the Battle of
North Point, a two-hour
delaying action by Ameri-
cans "who stood their ground
against a veteran British army,

FORT McHENRY.

The Fort McHenry rooster

was one of the few such actions of American soil south of
the Canadian theater of war." He adds, "Both certainly deserve better recognition."

Francis Scott Key, of course, had no notion of how the
battle for Baltimore was going. The British fleet continued
its bombardment of Fort McHenry to cover the withdrawal of the army, ending its attack at seven o'clock in
the morning of September 14 and sailing down the Patapsco two hours later. Legend has it that a rooster had
climbed onto the big flagpole during the attack and had
crowed its defiance at the British fleet. As a reward, it was
fed some pound cake and when it died—was it the pound

cake?—the rooster was buried with honors at the fort. On September 15, the withdrawing British army, its movements shielded by a heavy rain, reached North Point and went back aboard the ships. Two days later, the British fleet sailed off. The Americans had won at Baltimore.

Rear Admiral George Cockburn, the commander of the British naval forces in the march from North Point to Baltimore, regarded the expedition as a failure, but the failure did not seem to have affected his reputation or career. He is now remembered as the man who conveyed Napoleon to his final exile on St. Helena, Elba having failed to hold him, and was governor there for eighteen months. How does one baby-sit for the Little Corporal? An official history says of Cockburn: "On 15 Oct. [1815], he arrived at St. Helena, and having landed his prisoner, remained in the twofold character of governor of the island and commander in chief of the stations, the duties of which post were rendered extremely irksome by the necessity of unceasing vigilance."

While some credit Cockburn with the idea to attack the defenseless Washington, Sir George de Lacy Evans, who was General Ross's deputy quartermaster at Bladensburg, published a pamphlet in 1829 accusing Cockburn of claiming too much credit for the attack on Washington and alleging that he "used the death of Ross to inflate his own role." Ross himself was more generous toward his friend, writing, "To Rear Admiral Cockburn, who suggested the attack upon Washington, and who accompanied the army, I confess the greatest obligations for his cordial cooperation and advice." Cockburn called Baltimore a failure, but higher-ups tried to put it in a rosier light. The chancellor of the exchequer, Nicholas Vansittart, the first baron Bexley, told Parliament on November 14, 1814, that Ross's attack had been successful. In a letter to Earl Bathurst, a leading political figure of the day named Henry Goulburn wrote of receiving letters about the attack on Baltimore, saying, "The news which they brought from America is very far from satisfactory. Even our brilliant success at Baltimore, as it did not terminate in the capture of the town, will be considered by the Americans as a victory, and not as an escape." Indeed.

Praising Ross in his earlier Napoleonic battles, the chancellor painted a picture of a brave, if sometimes foolhardy, hero. "In the Battle of the Pyrenees," the chancellor said, "by his extraordinary abilities, drew down the particular thanks of the commander in chief, who, in speaking of Major General Ross's division, said, 'It had distinguished itself beyond all former precedent; it had charged four times, and each time was headed by the major general, who had three horses killed under him.'" The general was tough on horses.

"At the close of the war with France," the chancellor continued in his eulogy of Ross to Parliament, "he was one of those officers who were dispatched to America; and here, while he brought his renown to the highest pitch, he terminated his transcendent career. In conjunction with Admiral Cockburn, he planned that attack upon Washington, which, in defiance of the difficulties which were encountered, and the superiority of the enemy's force, was crowned with success. Major General Ross was, on this occasion, chosen to retaliate upon the Americans for the outrages which they had committed on the frontiers; and while he inflicted chastisement in a manner to convey, in the fullest manner, the terror of the British arms, the Americans themselves could not withhold from him the meed of praise, for the temper and moderation with which he executed the task assigned him. The public buildings alone were destroyed, while private property was in every instance respected." As already mentioned, it is an exaggeration to describe the American force as superior to the British. The Americans may have been greater in number but they were poorly equipped and not well trained. The British captured Washington with no difficulty at all.

One member of Parliament, named Whitshed Keene, told the House of Commons during the debate over raising a statue in Ross's honor that nothing the government could do would be able to make up for the loss of Ross. "He possessed the happy talent of conciliating by his disposition, and instructing by his example," Keene said. "He possessed, indeed, all those private and distinguished qualifications by which alone a commander could acquire the full confidence of his men."

Another parliamentarian, named Ponsonby, said, "There never lived a man who deserved more, or who had received more of the confidence and affection of those who served under him, than this lamented individual. Whether in the field, or elsewhere, he was alike distinguished for tenderness and gentleness. In private life there never lived a man more distinguished for social virtues, and for all the amiabilities of human nature." Ponsonby responded to the chancellor's words about Ross's attack on Washington, saying, "He was sorry that the gallant general had been selected as the individual to execute those plans of vengeance, which, he had hoped, had been abolished in civilized warfare. He did not mean to say that the Americans did not deserve punishment for the outrages of which they had been guilty; but he was sorry, in one sense, that the execution of that punishment should have fallen to General Ross as there never lived a man who would have felt more pain in executing such an order, unless impelled by necessity. In another sense, he was glad that he was chosen on this occasion, because he believed there was not a man in the British service who would have carried the order into execution in a manner less injurious or attended with less mischievous consequences." Finally, a member named C. Grant, Jr., declared that Ross's "name had been made sacred by his bravery and unfortunate end."

The question arises: If Ross had not been killed by the sniper's bullet, would the outcome at Baltimore been different? If the British had captured Baltimore, what effect would that have had on the outcome of the war? The earl of Liverpool said in a letter to Viscount Castlereagh that Britain had sent too many troops to Canada and not enough to the Chesapeake. Canada would have been safe with half the troops assigned to it, Liverpool wrote, "and I verily believe that with the remainder added to the force placed under the command of General Ross, we might have taken possession of every considerable town in America south of Philadelphia." The British had reassigned four brigades of infantry to North America after they defeated Napoleon. Three of the brigades were sent to Canada and the fourth was sent to attack America under Ross.

Ross had been seriously wounded in the Napoleonic wars. His unit captured the village of St. Boës and charged the French enemy five times in the face of artillery and musket fire, when he was hit. Two weeks later, he wrote, "You will be happy to hear that the hit I got in the chops is likely to prove of mere temporary inconvenience." His wife, Elizabeth, nursed him after his wound and when he went to America three months later, he promised her that it would be his last campaign. It was, although not in the way he envisioned it.

Vice Admiral Cochrane, who was in overall command in the region, said that the effort prompted the Americans to negotiate in peace-settlement talks at Ghent, by demonstrating that the British could land at will throughout the United States, and Cochrane's next order was to attack New Orleans.

7

Two Weary Nations Agree to End Their War

The British had offered to start peace negotiations in January 1814, and the United States accepted, sending Henry Clay, Albert Gallatin and John Quincy Adams to the talks in Ghent. Henry Goulburn, one of the British negotiators, said in a letter to a superior that "Gallatin appears to be the only American in any degree sensible, and perhaps this arises from his being less like an American than any of his colleagues," a comment that may show that the British still did not know who they were dealing with. The talks went on for a year, but the Americans were never able to win agreement from the British to halt the impressment of sailors. That meant little, since the defeat of Napoleon meant that Britain had little need to seize seamen and had discontinued doing it. Both sides were eager to end the war. Americans who had wanted to annex parts of Canada had largely given up that goal. The American economy was suffering because of paralysis of trade. Goulburn had written that the maritime issues had been raised falsely by the Americans and that they gave them up "as soon as they found the real object of the war, the conquest of Canada, unattainable." The British were also suffering economically and were weary of war.

John Murray, the British officer quoted earlier on the death of Ross, commented on the outcome of the war.

The fact is, however, that when we look back upon the whole series of events produced by the late American war, we shall find little that is likely to flatter our vanity, or increase our self-importance. Except a few successes in Canada, at its very commencement, and the brilliant inroad upon Washington, it will be found that our arms have been constantly baffled or repulsed on shore. . . . [H]ad ten thousand men sailed from Garonne under General Ross, how differently might he have acted! There would have been no necessity for re-embarkation after the capture of Washington, and consequently no time given for the defense of Baltimore; but marching across the country, he might have done to the one city what he did to the other. And it is thus only that a war with America can be successfully carried on. America must be assaulted only on her coasts. Her harbors destroyed, her shipping burned, and her seaport towns laid waste, are the only evils she has reason to dread. To the plan which I propose of making desert the whole line of coast. By compelling the constituents to experience the real hardships and miseries of warfare, you will soon compel the representatives to a vote of peace.

A peace treaty was signed on December 24, 1814, essentially restoring the status quo of 1812, but word of the agreement, traveling by ship, did not reach the United States until after the Battle of New Orleans. On January 8, 1815, the British attacked New Orleans, which was defended by a full melting-pot of soldiers forged into an army by General Andrew Jackson. There were frontier riflemen from Kentucky and Tennessee, regular army men, militia members, wellborn citizens of New Orleans, a unit called the New Orleans sharpshooters, Choctaw Indians, perhaps a thousand pirates serving under the lawless Jean Lafitte, and two battalions of free black soldiers. Theodore Roosevelt called attention to the irony of the black soldiers playing such an important role in the defense of the city against Britain, which had outlawed slavery in 1807. "One band had in its formation something that was curiously pathetic," Roosevelt wrote. "It was composed of free men of color, who had gathered to defend the land which kept the men of their race in slavery; who were to shed their blood for the Flag that symbolized to their kind not freedom but bondage; who were to die bravely as freemen, only that their brethren might live on ignobly as slaves. Surely there was never a stranger instance than this irony of fate."

When Jackson learned that the British planned to attack New Orleans, he said, "I will smash them, so help me God," and he did. It was a one-sided battle. The British suffered 2,057 dead, while the Americans had just 13 killed. As in other battles in the War of 1812, including the one at Baltimore, the commander of the British army forces was killed. General Sir Edward Pakenham, who was in command because of the death of General Ross, rode into battle to inspire his troops as they were being ripped apart by Jackson's men, and was shot down himself. The greatest soldier of that day, the duke of Wellington, who vanquished Napoleon and was Pakenham's brother-in-law, had written to a friend a few years earlier, "I begin to be of the opinion with you that there is nothing as stupid as a gallant officer."

John Quincy Adams, one of the American negotiators at Ghent and later the sixth president of the United States, and the son of John Adams, the second president, wrote in his biography of President James Madison: "The war was brought to a close without any definitive adjustment of the controversial principles in which it had originated. It left the questions of neutral commerce with an enemy and his colonies, of bottom and cargo, of blockade and contraband of war, and even of impressment, precisely as they had been before the war. With the European war all the conflicts between belligerent and neutral rights had ceased. Great Britain, triumphant as she was after a struggle of more than twenty years' duration—against revolutionary, republican and imperial France—was in no temper to yield the principles for which in the heat of her contest she had defied the power of neutrality and the voice of justice. As little were the Government or people of the United States disposed to yield principles in the defense of the rights of neutrality, and of conceding too much to the lawless pretensions of naval war."

The war ended as it had begun. In 1812, word of the British withdrawal of the Orders of Council, one of the principal causes of the war, arrived after the United States had declared war. Now word of the end of the war arrived too late to stop its biggest battle. After the treaty finally arrived in Washington, Congress approved it quickly and President Madison proclaimed the end of the war on February 17, 1815. Because New Orleans was such a great victory and came at the end of the war, many Americans were left with the impression that the United States had won. It had not. The war ended with neither victory nor defeat. It was known as the War Nobody Won—which may help explain why so few Americans know anything about it. But it had a singular effect. Albert Gallatin, one of the American negotiators, said after the peace treaty was signed that the war had made Americans "feel and act more like a nation," and he was right. America did not know it at the time, but it had become a nation. America had made the world realize that it was an emerging giant, and Britain never again interfered with

American shipping. In the next century, America would come to the rescue of Britain in two world wars, saving it from defeat.

Because of the War of 1812, industry flourished in the Northeast as Americans had to make many goods for the first time because commerce with Europe had been interrupted. And, not yet knowing it, America had gained a national anthem.

8

Where the Flag and the Song Went After the War

After the War of 1812, Lieutenant Colonel George Armi-stead, since promoted from major, who led the defense of Fort McHenry, took home the huge American flag that Mary Pickersgill had made. "It was either presented to him or he just took it," said Lonn Taylor, a historian at the Smithsonian Institution and an authority on the Star-Spangled Banner. "We have not found any documentation, but there probably is some because in government you have to write things down."

If the British had defeated the Americans at Fort McHenry, the commander of the British force would have carried off the flag as war booty. That's what happened at the Battle of Fort Niagara in New York, when the British defeated the Americans on the night of December 18–19,

1813, and captured the fort's flag. According to the Old Fort Niagara Association, the American lads made things rather easy for the British by leaving a gate partly open while the sentries were being changed, allowing the British force to rush in and overcome the sleeping American soldiers in the middle of the night. The fort's flag was taken first to Quebec and then to London, along with the captured American flags of Fort Mackinac in Michigan and Fort Ontario in Oswego, New York. All three were presented to the prince regent, later King George IV. The Niagara and Ontario flags were then given by the prince to Major General Sir Gordon Drummond, the British commander in Upper Canada. The flags were taken away to Drummond's castle in Scotland and the Niagara flag, at least, benefited by the flagnapping, since it was kept largely intact, hanging in a room inside the castle.

Until the Civil War, flags did not enjoy the iconic status that they have today, and they were not yet the objects of adoration in Fourth of July speeches by patriots sincere and false, and little attention was paid to preserving them whole as national symbols. Because of this inattention and neglect, the Fort Niagara and Fort McHenry flags are among the very few flags of the early days of the Republic that have survived. Indeed, the Old Fort Niagara Association says that its flag is one of only about twenty American flags from before 1815 known to exist. The last British owner of the Fort Niagara flag was the sixteenth baroness Strange, who, absent powdered wig, is also Mrs. Cherry Drummond. Her husband, Captain Humphrey Drum-

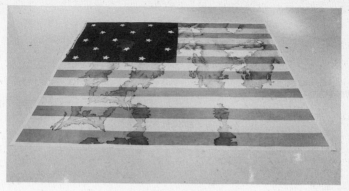

The Fort Niagra flag

mond, answered the phone when a call was made to their home, Megginch Castle, in Errol, Perthshire, Scotland, because she was in the House of Lords in London that day, doing whatever it is that the lords and ladies of Parliament do. Captain Drummond said yes, it was true, as the Fort Niagara people had said, that he had saved the flag from destruction during a fire in the castle in 1969. A building as big as a castle is needed to display a large flag like the one from Fort Niagara, and it had been put there by General Drummond, an ancestor of Baroness Strange—she is his great-great-grandniece. Lady Strange is president of the War Widows Association and is a long-standing campaigner for a law that allows the widows to keep their pensions if they remarry. Captain Drummond—he explained that he had adopted his wife's family name as his—risked his life to run into the castle during the fire and save the flag, but he said, "It wasn't as dramatic as that." His rescue dash showed that the Drummond family regarded the flag as very valuable, as the fire did damage half the castle. The flag suffered a loss of thirty-five to forty percent of its total in the fire, but Captain Drummond managed to save it and the family sold it in 1993 to the Old Fort Niagara Association in Youngstown, New York, for $150,000.

Deborah Trupin, textile conservator with the New York State Office of Parks, Recreation and Historic Preservation, said, "It is a fifteen-star and fifteen-stripe flag, but we don't know who made it. It's wool with a linen header and stars," the header being the strip of cloth that lets the flag run up the flagpole, like the one at Fort McHenry. The flag is a garrison flag and big by most standards, twenty-four feet high and now, after the fire, reduced to twenty-eight feet long, but much smaller than the Fort McHenry flag. The Fort Niagara flag was placed on display in a temporary exhibition in 1995 and then put into storage, where it remains. The Old Fort Niagara Association, which raised the money to buy it, would like to have scientific analysis performed on it someday if the money can be found. "A limited budget has so far precluded the commissioning of scientific analysis," Ms. Trupin said. Absent the money for research, no analysis has been done on the dyes used. Like the Fort McHenry flag, the Niagara flag is made of wool bunting in an open weave to reduce weight. The white stripes on the Niagara flag have darkened and the red stripes have faded, but according to the Old Fort Niagara Association, the blue field and white stars retain their original brilliance. As was the case with Mary Pickers-gill's flag in Baltimore, the unknown maker of the Niagara flag, instead of producing fifteen stars for each side, applied fifteen stars on one side, then turned over the flag and cut out fifteen star-shaped holes from the blue field, making each star do the work of two. This was evidently a common practice at the time, necessitated by the high cost of textiles. The flag has a number of large holes, some caused by the fire in the castle in 1969. The flag is somewhat brittle, especially at the edges of the fire damage, and since the fire the fabric has undergone conservation. It is about as stable as an historic fabric of its age can be.

"The wiring was very old," Captain Drummond said in describing the fire at the castle. "The place was rewired three months before it burst into flames. We did what we could."

Besides the damage from the fire, the Niagara flag had suffered some losses ascribed to what textile historians gently describe as "souveniring," that is, people taking pieces of it, a common nineteenth-century practice. The same "souveniring" has had a big impact on the Star-Spangled Banner, according to Suzanne Thomassen-Krauss, the chief conservator for the Star-Spangled Banner Preservation Project and senior textile conservator for the National Museum of American History. After the Battle of Fort McHenry, legend has it that the widow of a veteran of the bombardment asked Armistead for a piece of the flag as a remembrance or to be buried with him, and one version even suggests that she was the widow of someone actually killed there. "I am not sure where the story about the widow asking for a piece of the flag for her husband to be buried in comes from," said Lonn Taylor, the author of *The Star-Spangled Banner: The Flag That Inspired the National Anthem*. "I have read the obituaries of two of the men killed, Claggett and Clemm, and no mention is made of a piece of the flag being buried with them. The earliest appearance of this story that I have found in print is in an article in the *New York Herald* of August 4, 1895, signed by Mrs. George Livingston Baker, who was one of George Armistead's granddaughters. There is a good deal of misinformation in this article, and I have found no documentation of this story elsewhere, so in my book I simply describe it as an Armistead family tradition. The *Herald* article says that Mrs. Baker remembers 'hearing from my mother that a brave soldier who had served under her father on his deathbed wrote and requested Mrs. Armistead to let him have a piece to wrap around his dead body.' So in that story, at least, it was not a soldier who was killed in the battle but a veteran who died at some later date. There are a number of stories like this that appear in newspapers in the 1880s and '90s that cannot be documented, probably a reflection of the journalistic standards of the time."

Because intact American flags had not yet reached the state of almost religious adoration that is lavished on them today, it was standard military practice up until the Civil War to remove sections of flags for the families of soldiers killed while fighting for it and the nation. A little bit here, a little bit there, and before you know it a piece of a very large flag is gone. A very large piece. The Star-Spangled Banner, once forty-two by thirty feet, had been reduced to thirty-three by thirty feet by the time the practice was halted early in the twentieth century. "Taking a piece probably became a tradition," said Ronald E. Becker, a Smithsonian Institution official involved in conserving the flag. "We figure that when it was hung from buildings, people came by and took a hunk." Seven of those hunks are in the Star-Spangled Banner Flag House in Baltimore. When I visited the museum, three swatches, each about four inches square—one red, one white and one blue, of course—were on display in a clear plastic, star-shaped display case, and the red piece has a line of stitches that the flag museum likes to imagine may have been sewn by Mary Pickersgill, but there is no way of being certain of that. The display struck me as a secular version of the reliquaries with saints' bones or splinters of the true cross on display in European cathedrals.

In 1873, when George Preble received permission to photograph the flag, it had reached the condition that it is in today. "One of the stars was missing," Thomassen-Krauss said. "It had already been souvenired by then. She said that Preble stitched the Star-Spangled Banner to a stiff canvas backing, which was still attached when the flag came to the Smithsonian Institution in 1907. Taylor writes that Preble, who became a great publicist for the flag, got permission from Major Armistead's daughter, Georgiana Armistead Appleton, to cut some pieces of the Star-Spangled Banner for display with copies of his

*Earliest known photograph of the Star-Spangled Banner,
at Boston Navy Yard, 1874.*

photograph. The flag was displayed in what used to be
known as the Smithsonian's Arts and Industries Building
until 1963, when it was moved to the Smithsonian's newly
opened division, the National Museum of American History, on the Mall in Washington.

No one knows who got the single star that is missing
from the Star-Spangled Banner and is represented today

by a later embroidery. Georgiana wrote in a letter that "the star was cut out for some official person," but she does not identify who it was. But Taylor, the Smithsonian expert, thinks he has solved another mystery—the presence of the letter V in red on one of the white stripes. The answer, Taylor thinks, is that it is not a V at all. "I think it is an A without the crossbar," Taylor said. "It was either never on or it fell off." And what does the A stand for? Armistead, of course, Taylor says. Georgiana wrote, "The red letter A was presumably sewn on by my mother." In addition, Major Armistead is thought to have signed his name in two places, according to a 1914 account, but this has not been confirmed.

Armistead died of pneumonia in 1818 at the age of thirty-eight, and the flag passed into the possession of his widow, Louisa. According to research by Scott S. Sheads and Anna von Lunz of the Fort McHenry National Monument, Louisa Armistead lent her "precious relic" for a ceremony at the fort in October 1824 honoring the marquis de Lafayette, the French aristocrat who served as a military aide to George Washington during the Revolutionary War. "This memorable occasion marked the flag's first appearance at Fort McHenry since the battle and the last time the banner would ever wave from the historic flag's flagstaff," Sheads and von Lunz wrote in the *Maryland Historical Magazine*.

The flag stayed in Louisa Armistead's possession until her death in 1861, when it descended to her daughter, Georgiana Armistead Appleton. In 1876, it was sent to

Philadelphia for display at the nation's centennial celebration, and Georgiana bequeathed it to her son, Eben Appleton. This Appleton kept it in a bank vault in Manhattan, lent it for display during a celebration in Baltimore, and then returned it to the bank vault, but not before letting a Baltimorean snip red, white and blue fragments from the flag. In 1907, Appleton lent it to the Smithsonian Institution. He converted the loan to a gift in 1912, and it has been in the Smithsonian's possession ever since.

During World War II, the Smithsonian stored the flag and several other important artifacts in a safe place near the Luray Caverns in Virginia. From 1944 until 1963, it was displayed in the Smithsonian's Arts and Industries Building, and it has been in its present home, the Smithsonian's National Museum of American History, since 1963.

In 1914, the Smithsonian conducted the first preservation project for the Star-Spangled Banner, and Amelia Fowler, who was commissioned to lead it, mounted the flag on a linen backing and trained groups of seamstresses to work on it. Her system was to hold the flag in place against the linen with twelve to fourteen stitches of linen thread per square inch, to a point that 1,700,000 stitches held the flag onto the backing. All those stitches created a netlike effect on the flag, sort of a haze that people could not quite see but that prevented the flag from being seen clearly. When Thomassen-Krauss's team of conservators removed the stitching from the first one-square-foot section in 1999, they saw a red stripe in a color much truer than at any time since the stitching was done. Was it a

Enlargement of dirt on the Star-Spangled Banner

good idea to sew on the linen in 1914? "Yes, it was," Thomassen-Krauss said. "At the time, it was about the best material to use. The problem was that they dyed the linen stitching, and linen doesn't hold dye very well. As the red and blue threads aged and the dye faded, you could see the stitching."

As part of a conservation project that began in 1999, the Smithsonian Institution is trying to decide what to do once the linen is removed. The linen backing and, before that, the canvas, covered one side of the Star-Spangled Banner, and a flag is meant to be seen from both sides. It doesn't have a front and a back, a heads and a tails. It has two fronts. "Ideally," Thomassen-Krauss said, "we would want people to be able to see both sides. Flags are intended to have two faces—it is paintings and prints that have only one face. We have a lot of options. Somebody has suggested the world's largest showcase. It would be the size of the façade of a three-story building." Washington seems to have institutionalized the notion of multiple fronts. Neither the White House nor the Capitol has a back door. The White House has a ceremonial entrance and a diplomatic entrance; the Capitol has a West Front and an East Front.

The conservation of textiles, if one may reduce a discussion of the Star-Spangled Banner to such a mundane term, is a tricky business. Light damages wool very quickly, and light was not the only thing that harmed the Star-Spangled Banner. It has been damaged by exposure to ultraviolet light and oxygen, and it has been exposed to dirt from an enormous variety of sources. "We had a photograph, at five hundred times magnification, that showed pollen grains, clay, fibers," Thomassen-Krauss said. "One of my colleagues said it looked like Bourbon Street after Mardi Gras." There is a myth that denim, shed in microscopic amounts by the blue jeans of millions of visitors to the museum, constituted a major part of the dirt, but Thomassen-Krauss said that few of those fibers were found. Every time the doors opened to let people in or out, whiffs of oily air from passing cars, trucks and buses made their way into the museum, some of it winding up on the flag. There are lubricating oils in the museum's elevators and escalators, and tiny bits of fine mists from them found their way to the flag. Other particles consisted of bits of grass and leaves, fibrous debris from cotton cloths and buffing pads used to clean the building and stray fibers from clothing. A little here, a little there, and you end with a dirty flag. And then there are cracks. "As textiles age, the surface of the fibers will begin to crack because of frequent flexing and bending," Thomassen-Krauss said. In 1982, the Star-Spangled Banner was vacuumed in place, lightly, so as to not damage the fabric, as it hung in the Smithsonian's National Museum of American History. Anyone who has had woolen clothing damaged by moths will be surprised to learn that the Star-Spangled Banner has not been harmed by them. The reason is that for years the flag has been protected against insects by flakes or mothballs made of para-dichlorobenzene and napthalene, which had to be used with care because they are a central-nervous-system depressant. Pesticides are no longer used and the museum suspects that some other insects did cause some damage.

In 1999, the first year of the new conservation project, the Smithsonian's workers snipped each one of those 1,700,000 stitches that were holding the flag to the linen backing. Then the huge flag, its backing still there, was put back on a big roller to prepare it for turning over so that it could be rolled out again and the linen backing lifted. At this point, the estimated weight was about one hundred thirty-five pounds, much of that from the linen backing.

Lonn Taylor, who is the historian for the flag preservation project at the Smithsonian, remarked that "a lot of our visitors did not know that there was a flag that inspired 'The Star-Spangled Banner.'" "Although that may change with the attention brought on by the preservation project, and maybe, modestly, this book, as well as Taylor's, he was right when he spoke. For years the flag hung behind the swaying shaft of a pendulum that showed, if you had the patience, that the earth rotates, and I once spent half an hour there and perhaps two or three of the dozens of visitors to that part of the museum walked over to see the Star-Spangled Banner. One reason, I think, is that the flag is so big that the ordinary person did not see it as a flag. If that person saw anything, it was a wall of red and white stripes. Perhaps the Smithsonian will come up with a solution to this problem of hiding a massive object in plain sight.

Taylor is filled with admiration of the family that preserved the flag for the nation, the descendants of Lieutenant Colonel Armistead. "The flag was preserved in private hands for so long," he said, "and the woman primarily responsible was not wealthy and could have sold the flag in the 1870s. She wrote a letter saying that she would rather beg than part with her treasure." Taylor was referring to Armistead's daughter, Georgiana Armistead Appleton, who lived in Baltimore, New York and Boston. "She held on to it and took it with her when she moved," Taylor said.

There is a handwritten inscription on one of the stars

that says, "This precious relic of my father's fame I," and then there is a hole where the balance of the inscription would have been, followed by the signature "Georgiana Armistead Appleton" and the date June 24, 1876. "I think she sent the flag to the Centennial exhibition in Philadelphia in 1876 or to a museum and then changed her mind," said Taylor, who has made a study of the whereabouts of the great flag. "She was a Southern sympathizer in the Civil War. Her son, George Armistead Appleton, was arrested while trying to cross into Virginia with a Confederate flag in his possession. He was imprisoned in Fort McHenry on treason charges." An interesting turn of fate there, especially since it happened on September 12, 1861, Defenders Day, the holiday that Baltimore celebrates annually to mark the defense of their city. Fort McHenry was used by Union forces during the Civil War as a prison camp for the detention of Confederate soldiers, Southern sympathizers and political prisoners. Also arrested that same Defenders Day in 1861 was a grandson of Francis Scott Key, Frank Key Howard, editor of *The Baltimore Exchange*, a pro-Southern newspaper. Howard was also imprisoned at Fort McHenry in what Scott S. Sheads and Anna von Lunz described as "extreme irony" as they recorded his account of his ordeal in a pamphlet called *An American Bastille*:

When I looked out in the morning, I could not help being struck by an odd and not so pleasant coincidence. On that day, forty-seven years before, my grandfather, Mr. F. S. Key, then a prisoner on a British ship, had witnessed the bombardment of Fort McHenry. When on the following morning, the hostile fleet drew off, defeated, he wrote the song so long popular throughout the country, the "Star-Spangled Banner." As I stood upon the very scene of that conflict, I could not but contrast my position with his, forty-seven years before. The flag which he had then so proudly hailed, I saw waving, at the same place, over the victims of as vulgar and brutal a despotism as modern times have witnessed.

Maryland was in an awkward position during the Civil War since, while it was officially aligned with the Union, the hearts of many were with the South, and the location of Washington, D.C., in what had once been a part of Maryland, made it especially important for the North to keep it well garrisoned with Union soldiers. Although the South did attack Maryland to the west of Washington, notably at Antietam, it did not go after Baltimore, which is to the east.

Slowly, little by little, the flag and the song were set deeper into our national consciousness. The song grew in popularity from the mid–nineteenth century onward, attracting a larger following among the military in the Civil War—from both the Northern and Southern forces.

9

Little by Little, America Gets a National Anthem

During our lifetimes, "The Star-Spangled Banner" has been the only national anthem we have known, but it is a relatively recent habit. During the 1890s it was adopted as the official song of both the army and the navy, and it got another boost during the Spanish-American War.

The practice of playing a country's national anthem and raising its flag for the winner of an event at the Olympics has become so ingrained in the public mind that most people probably think that this has always been done. Hokey movies aside, this is not the case. According to the United States Olympic Committee, the first time that the national anthems were played and the national flags raised during the victory ceremonies was at the 1932 Olympics in Los Angeles. The practice is regrettable. Instead of celebrating one *athlete's* victory over another in fair competition, which is laudable, this part of the Olympics leads to a compilation that proclaims one *country's* supposed superiority. Too much nationalism can be a bad thing—witness Hitler's attempts to use the 1936 Olympics in Berlin as a stage to try to show the purported superiority of his so-called Aryan race. Luckily it backfired when many black American athletes won. Attempts by the former East Germany and other Communist countries to push their athletes into what were essentially sports factories were to show the alleged superiority of their political system during the Cold War. Today the only thing they have to show for their political system is a collection of gold medals.

Professor William Guegold of the University of Akron, a leading authority on music at the Olympics and director of his college's School of Music, says that there are anecdotes that speak of performances of national anthems when the games were reinstituted in Athens in 1896. One story—thus far unproved—is that one of the American athletes said that the importance of his achievement in winning a gold medal really hit home during the awards ceremony. An American warship, Guegold said in relating the tale, was in the harbor at the time and attended the ceremonies, and the athlete remarked that he was very touched and proud when all of the sailors came to attention and saluted when the national anthem was played at the raising of the American flag. In those days, all of the medals were awarded in one large ceremony instead of after each event, the modern practice. Guegold, the author of *100 Years of Olympic Music*, is continuing his research for a new edition of his book and hopes to determine if there is any basis at all in that story.

By 1904, the song was so closely identified with the United States abroad that Giacomo Puccini used it as a theme in his opera *Madama Butterfly* to introduce Lieutenant Pinkerton, the faithless American naval officer who is to marry and desert the innocent Japanese maiden Cio-Cio-San. Puccini knew that his audience at La Scala in Milan would connect the song to the United States.

In 1916, President Woodrow Wilson ordered that it be played on official occasions, and America's entrance into World War I enhanced its patriotic aura. Finally, Congress passed a law, signed by President Herbert Hoover on March 3, 1931, making "The Star-Spangled Banner" officially our national anthem. This did not occur overnight. The Library of Congress has reckoned that more than forty bills and joint resolutions were introduced during a twenty-year effort, led by the Veterans of Foreign Wars and other veteran, patriotic and civic organizations, before the song was adopted. In 1930, the VFW announced that it had obtained five million signatures on a petition urging that "The Star-Spangled Banner" be declared the national anthem. Its main competitors, which, of course, were to lose out, were "America the Beautiful" and "Yankee Doodle," which by a turn of fate was the song played in victory after the Americans at Fort McHenry successfully fought off the British in the Baltimore battle that inspired Francis Scott Key to write "The Star-Spangled Banner."

Why was there opposition? Some people found "The Star-Spangled Banner" inappropriate because the campaign to adopt it as the national anthem came during Prohibition, and its opponents pointed out that the tune was from an old drinking song. Prohibition was imposed in 1919 with the Eighteenth Amendment to the Constitution, an action that confirms further the wisdom of resisting changes in that great document. Repeal of Prohibition came with the Twenty-first Amendment in 1933. In addition, the opponents criticized it on the ground that the music was foreign—English, no less—and therefore inappropriate for America's national anthem. Some people objected that the song was too difficult to sing because of its wide vocal range, a complaint that anyone without vocal training can understand. If we can reach the low notes, we can't hit the high ones. The *New York Herald Tribune* summed up things nicely, saying that "The Star-Spangled Banner" had "words that nobody can remember to a tune that nobody can sing."

Two sopranos, Elsie Jorss-Reilley of Washington and Grace Evelyn Boudlin of Baltimore, sang "The Star-Spangled Banner" at a congressional hearing on January 31, 1930, in an attempt to persuade its members that the song was not as the *Herald Tribune* and others had made it out to be. They were accompanied by the navy band in their odd performance, which was held before the House Judiciary Committee and an audience of advocates, many of them members of women's organizations wearing broad ribbons in red, white and blue. Captain Walter I. Joyce, commander in chief of the Veterans of Foreign Wars, told the committee that, whatever course Congress took, the former soldiers, sailors and marines of his organization would always regard "The Star-Spangled Banner" as their national anthem. Whether it was the sopranos, the Navy bandsmen or the veterans, the Judiciary Committee reported the bill out favorably on February 4 and sent it to the floor of the House of Representatives, which passed it on April 21, 1930. The Senate gave final legislative passage to the bill on March 3, 1931, and President Hoover signed it later that day.

Albert S. Bard was clearly swimming against the tide when he wrote this thoughtful letter to the editor of *The New York Times* in 1930 opposing the anthem bill, one of whose principal sponsors was Representative J. Charles Linthicum of Maryland:

I hope that Congress will not pass the Linthicum bill to make "The Star-Spangled Banner" the national anthem.

My reason is not that the old English song which furnishes the music, and was popular in its day, was once a convivial drinking song. The music has outgrown that undignified stage. It is no longer popular in that sense, if it is in any sense, and is today known solely in connection with the Francis Scott Key words. The musical reason is that the music is ill adapted to a national anthem, which should be of moderate range, to be compassed by ordinary voices. If "The Star-Spangled Banner" music is transposed as to take the edge off the high notes, the low notes are too low for beauty and dignity of effect. Nor has the music the simple beauty and grandeur to express properly the soul of a great people, as our national anthem should have.

But worse than the music are the words of Key's poem. They expressed the stock feeling of the time toward a then enemy. Today both the sentiment and language are outmoded and seem rather silly. About all that can be said for them is that they are probably somewhat better than that paragon of absurdity, the British national anthem and its "knavish tricks." [The reference is to a section from "God Save the King (Queen)" that says: *O Lord, our God, arise,/Scatter our enemies/And make them fail./Compound their politics,/Frustrate their knavish tricks.*]

Naturally Representative Linthicum of Maryland would like to see a Maryland incident of no great importance in national history embalmed in the national anthem. People feel that way about their own little affairs. But cannot the nation have some sense of proportion?

If we are to have a national anthem adopted by act of Congress the words of Katharine Lee Bates's "America the Beautiful" are far more like what we want and need.

The thing that has made "The Star-Spangled Banner" live so long as it has is the poetry in the line which gives the poem its name, plus the head start it got through the use of its music by government bands in default of anything better. "The Star-Spangled Banner" is not good enough for the real America. Let us try again.

Opposition to adoption of "The Star-Spangled Banner" also came from education experts at Columbia University's Teachers College on the ground that its stimulating martial flavor was appropriate to wartime but should not be taught to the children of a nation at peace. This was in 1930, just twelve years after the end of what President Woodrow Wilson had called the war to end all wars. Little did they know then that the next great war was just a few years away. People were hopeful that the world would remain at peace. Peter W. Dykem, a professor of music education at the college, agreed with the prevalent view that "The Star-Spangled Banner" ranked with France's "Marseillaise" among great national anthems but that it required "a feeling of danger" to be sung properly. "The national anthem must be sung even when there is no crisis," Dykem said. " 'The Star-Spangled Banner' is an occasional song like some great operatic aria. When it is not sung on an occasion of national stress, like a declaration of war, it falls flat." A professor in the college's elementary education department, M. B. Hillegas, asserted that "The

Star-Spangled Banner" inspired a narrow type of patriotism, saying:

> It gives to millions of children who sing it the
> notion that the only real patriotism is warlike ac-
> tivity. No one questions the beauty and the power
> of "The Star-Spangled Banner." There are occa-
> sions when this stirring song should be sung, but
> these are not everyday occasions. The schools have
> been and are under severe criticism for their failure
> to make children understand that those activities
> which must be carried on day after day also have
> their patriotic aspects. Real patriotism must be as
> much concerned with peace as it is with war.
>
> Just so long as "The Star-Spangled Banner" is
> made the symbol of patriotism, just so long will it be
> difficult to convey to children the broader ideals of
> patriotism—love of home, neighborliness, good citi-
> zenship, pride in worthy accomplishment, regard
> for those great builders who have made our coun-
> try what it is and an eagerness to emulate them.
> These elements are found in Katharine Lee Bates's
> "America the Beautiful." If we have an official na-
> tional anthem, it should be one whose effect upon
> the mental and spiritual development of our chil-
> dren will be in keeping with real patriotism.

Clyde R. Miller, an administrator at Teachers College,
supported the adoption of "America the Beautiful" and said:

Surely no one questions the sincerity and good faith of those organizations which are urging the adoption of "The Star-Spangled Banner" as our national anthem, but I doubt if they have given any thought to the fact that this song offers a wholly one-sided idea of patriotism. It is making millions of schoolchildren believe that patriotism comes only in the crisis of war and that there must be a war or a serious threat of war before one can reveal one's patriotism.

"The Star-Spangled Banner" suggests that patriotism is associated with killing and being killed, with great noise and clamor, with intense hatreds and fury and violence. Patriotism may on very rare occasions involve all of these, but not everyday life. The Department of School Administration of Teachers College has for many years emphasized the importance of teaching constructive patriotism through music. Members of this department seem agreed that no better patriotic song has been written than "America the Beautiful." If the United States is to have a national anthem, it should be a song to promote the constructive patriotism of peace. The schools will do their share if war comes. But war will be less likely to come if an adequate patriotism is created by the schools.

Some of the opposition to "The Star-Spangled Banner" came from people who objected to the warlike tone of the third stanza, in which the normally pious, churchgoing Key, who opposed the War of 1812 in the first place, uncharacteristically condemns the British invaders:

And where is that band who so vauntingly swore
That the havoc of war and the battle's confusion
A home and a country should leave us no more?
Their blood has wash'd out their foul footsteps' pollution.
No refuge could save the hireling and slave
From the terror of flight or the gloom of the grave:
And the star-spangled banner in triumph doth wave
O'er the land of the free and the home of the brave.

The question today is rather moot. When was the last time you heard the third stanza sung? Or any stanza other than the first? "Largely because of its warlike atmosphere," T. R. Ybarra wrote in *The New York Times* in 1931, "Key's composition has been the object of furious attacks for many years." He continued:

The words of the much-criticized song have been called too bellicose and too bumptious; the music has been branded as inappropriate and, above all, utterly unsuitable, since some of it lies beyond the range of the average voice. Despite these and other objections, "The Star-Spangled Banner" now stands at the head of the list—above "America" and "Hail, Columbia" and the legion of songs launched by ambitious American versifiers and composers in the fond hope that their work would be proclaimed our national anthem.

There is no gainsaying that "The Star-Spangled Banner" breathes a warlike spirit. Lovers of peace can derive little satisfaction from it. If it expresses the true attitude of Americans, we are indeed a nation which would raise an awful rumpus if anybody put up to it the proposition of turning swords into plowshares.

But even more vehement have been the objections caused by its alleged impoliteness. Written during the War of 1812, when passions were hot, it hurls at the British words which some people born in days of more restraint, have deemed insulting to a nation no longer our enemy.

All of those objecting to adoption of "The Star-Spangled Banner" as the national anthem raised valid points, but in the end Congress approved it and President Hoover signed it. Since then, there have been attempts made to have a different song declared the national anthem—"God Bless America" has its following—but they seem unlikely to succeed.

10

Should the Constitution Be Changed to Protect the Flag?

Should anyone think that the symbolic power of the flag is ancient history, a relic from a bygone age, think again. Over the years, there have been periodic attempts made to make the desecration of the American flag a crime. Veterans who have fought wars under its colors have recoiled as other citizens have burned the flag to make a political point. People who remember the protests over the war in Vietnam can attest to this. On the other side are the advocates of free speech, guaranteed by the First Amendment to the Constitution, who insist that the power of the flag is theirs as well. In one of the unresolved arguments in American society today, the question arises: Who owns the flag? If, as the Supreme Court has ruled, the Constitution protects flag burning as a form of free speech, should the Constitution be changed? The process of amending the Constitution is cumbersome and slow, a system that has served the country well by preventing hasty change. Our Constitution, besides being the oldest in the world, is also the most concise.

In the on-and-off debates in Congress, there have been sincere speakers on both sides, and clearly there have also been the sunshine patriots who, having seen that there is some gain to be made, have proclaimed their devotion to the flag so loudly that no one can fail to have heard them. They are playing to those prone to be easily led, those referred to by H. L. Mencken, the Baltimore sage and cynic, as the booboisie. One should always accept the opportunity to quote Mencken, who wrote in a discussion of American manners, for example, of "the unending procession of governmental extortions and chicaneries, of commercial brigandages and throat-slittings, of theological buffooneries, of aesthetic ribaldries, of legal swindles and harlotries, of miscellaneous rogueries, villainies, imbecilities, grotesqueries and extravagances."

At issue today is a decision by the United States Supreme Court, which ruled in 1989 by the narrowest of margins, five to four, that flag burning was a legitimate form of political expression. This was not a conservative-versus-liberal decision, and indeed, the notion of protecting the freedom of speech cannot easily be pigeonholed in that manner, although those members of Congress who say they favor an amendment to the Constitution that would allow laws punishing flag burning generally call themselves conservative.

The majority opinion was written by Justice William J. Brennan, Jr., one of the leading liberals on the Supreme Court. He was joined by Justice Thurgood Marshall, Brennan's staunchest liberal ally; Harry A. Blackmun, a moderate; and two conservatives, Antonin Scalia and Anthony M. Kennedy. Chief Justice William H. Rehnquist, a conservative, wrote the principal dissenting opinion, maintaining that the government could punish those who desecrate the flag, and was joined by two other conservatives, Justices Byron R. White and Sandra Day O'Connor. Justice John Paul Stevens, who usually could have been counted as a liberal ally of Brennan's, wrote a dissenting opinion, agreeing that flag burning could be punished. The case before the Supreme Court, *Texas* v. *Johnson*, was based on the case against Gregory L. Johnson, who was convicted of violating a Texas flag desecration law in 1984 during the Republican National Convention in Dallas. The act itself was not in dispute, as Justice Brennan wrote in his majority decision. "The demonstration ended in front of Dallas City Hall, where Johnson unfurled the American flag, doused it with kerosene, and set it on fire. While the flag burned, the protesters chanted, 'America, the red, white and blue, we spit on you.' After the demonstration dispersed, a witness to the flag burning collected the flag's remains and buried them in his backyard. No one was physically injured or threatened with injury, though several witnesses testified that they had been seriously offended by the flag burning. Of the approximately one hundred demonstrators, Johnson alone was charged with a crime. The only criminal offense with which he was charged was the desecration of a venerated object in violation of the Texas Penal Code. After a trial, he was convicted, sentenced to one year in prison and fined two thousand dollars. The Court of Appeals for the Fifth District of Texas at Dallas affirmed Johnson's conviction, but the Texas Court of Criminal Appeals reversed it, holding that the state could not, consistent with the First Amendment, punish Johnson for burning the flag in these circumstances."

The language of the opinions was colorful, and Brennan and Stevens emphasized the importance of the case—and their strong feelings about it—by reading their opinions aloud in the Supreme Court chambers instead of just having them announced and letting interested parties read them themselves. Excerpts from the decisions follow, with deletions indicated by ellipses.

JUSTICE BRENNAN'S
MAJORITY OPINION

After publicly burning an American flag as a means of political protest, Gregory Lee Johnson was convicted of desecrating a flag in violation of Texas law. This case presents the question whether his conviction is consistent with the First Amendment. We hold that it is not.

While the Republican National Convention was taking place in Dallas in 1984, respondent Johnson participated in a political demonstration dubbed "Republican War Chest Tour." As explained in literature distributed by the demonstrators and in speeches made by them, the purpose of this event was to protest the policies of the Reagan administration and of certain Dallas-based corporations. The demonstrators marched through the Dallas streets, chanting political slogans and stopping at several corporate locations to stage "die-ins" intended to dramatize the consequences of nuclear war. On several occasions they spray-painted the walls of buildings and overturned potted plants, but Johnson himself took no part in such activities. He did, however, accept an American flag handed to him by a fellow protestor who had taken it from a flagpole outside one of the targeted buildings. . . .

The Court of Criminal Appeals began by recognizing that Johnson's conduct was symbolic speech protected by the First Amendment: "Given the context of organized demonstrations, speeches, slogans and the distribution of literature, anyone who observed appellant's act would have understood the message that appellant intended to convey. The act for which appellant was convicted was clearly 'speech' contemplated by the First Amendment."

To justify Johnson's conviction for engaging in symbolic speech, the State asserted two interests: preserving the flag as a symbol of national unity and preventing breaches of the peace. The Court of Criminal Appeals held that neither interest supported his conviction.

Acknowledging that this Court had not yet decided whether the Government may criminally sanction flag desecration in order to preserve the flag's symbolic value, the Texas court nevertheless concluded that our decision in *West Virginia Board of Education* v. *Barnette* ... suggested that furthering this interest by curtailing speech was impermissible. "Recognizing that the right to differ is the centerpiece of our First Amendment freedoms," the court explained, "a government cannot mandate by fiat a feeling of unity in its citizens. Therefore, that very same government cannot carve out a symbol of unity and prescribe a set of approved messages to be associated with that symbol when it cannot mandate the status or feeling the symbol purports to represent." ...

As to the State's goal of preventing breaches of the peace, the court concluded that the flag desecration statute was not drawn narrowly enough to encompass only those flag burnings that were likely to result in a serious disturbance of the peace. And in fact, the court emphasized, the flag burning in this particular case did not threaten such a reaction.

" 'Serious offense' occurred," the court admitted, "but there was no breach of peace, nor does the record reflect that the situation was potentially explosive. One cannot equate 'serious offense' with incitement to breach the peace." . . .

The First Amendment literally forbids the abridgement only of "speech," but we have long recognized that its protection does not end at the spoken or written word. While we have rejected the view that an apparently limitless variety of conduct can be labeled "speech" whenever the person engaging in the conduct intends thereby to express an idea, we have acknowledged that conduct may be "sufficiently imbued with elements of communication to fall within the scope of the First and Fourteenth Amendments."

In deciding whether particular conduct possesses sufficient communicative elements to bring the First Amendment into play, we have asked whether "an intent to convey a particularized message was present and [whether] the likelihood was great that the message would be understood by those who viewed it." . . . Hence, we have recognized the expressive nature of students' wearing of black armbands to protest American involvement in Vietnam . . . ; of a sit-in by blacks in a "whites only" area to protest segregation . . . ; of the wearing of American military uniforms in a dramatic presentation criticizing

American involvement in Vietnam . . . ; and of pick-
eting about a wide variety of causes. . . .

Especially pertinent to this case are our decisions recognizing the communicative nature of
conduct relating to flags. Attaching a peace sign to
the flag . . . saluting the flag . . . and displaying a
red flag . . . we have held, all may find shelter under
the First Amendment (treating flag "contemptu-
ously" by wearing pants with a small flag sewn into
their seat is expressive conduct). That we have had
little difficulty identifying an expressive element in
conduct relating to flags should not be surprising.
The very purpose of a national flag is to serve as a
symbol of our country; it is, one might say, "the one
visible manifestation of two hundred years of nationhood. . . . Thus, we have observed: "The flag salute
is a form of utterance. Symbolism is a primitive but
effective way of communicating ideas. The use of
an emblem or flag to symbolize some system, idea,
institution or personality is a shortcut from mind to
mind. Causes and nations, political parties, lodges
and ecclesiastical groups seek to knit the loyalty
of their followings to a flag or banner, a color or
design."

Pregnant with expressive content, the flag as
readily signifies this nation as does the combination
of letters found in "America."

We have not automatically concluded, however,

that any action taken with respect to our flag is expressive. Instead, in characterizing such action for First Amendment purposes, we have considered the context in which it occurred. . . . The State of Texas conceded for purposes of its oral argument in this case that Johnson's conduct was expressive conduct. . . . Johnson burned an American flag as part—indeed, as the culmination—of a political demonstration that coincided with the convening of the Republican Party and its renomination of Ronald Reagan for President. The expressive, overtly political nature of this conduct was both intentional and overwhelmingly apparent. At his trial, Johnson explained his reasons for burning the flag as follows: "The American flag was burned as Ronald Reagan was being renominated as President. And a more powerful statement of symbolic speech, whether you agree with it or not, couldn't have been made at that time. It's quite a [juxtaposition]. We had new patriotism and no patriotism." . . . In these circumstances, Johnson's burning of the flag was "sufficiently imbued with elements of communication" . . . to implicate the First Amendment.

The Government generally has a freer hand in restricting expressive conduct than it has in restricting the written or spoken word. . . . It may not, however, proscribe particular conduct because it has expressive elements. . . . It is, in short, not simply the verbal or nonverbal nature of the expression, but the governmental interest at stake, that helps to determine whether a restriction on that expression is valid.

The State offers two separate interests to justify this conviction: preventing breaches of the peace, and preserving the flag as a symbol of nationhood and national unity. We hold that the first interest is not implicated on this record and that the second is related to the suppression of expression.

Texas claims that its interest in preventing breaches of the peace justifies Johnson's conviction for flag desecration. . . . However, no disturbance of the peace actually occurred or threatened to occur because of Johnson's burning of the flag. Although the state stresses the disruptive behavior of the protestors during their march toward City Hall . . . it admits that "no actual breach of the peace occurred at the time of the flag burning or in response to the flag burning. . . ." The state's position, therefore, amounts to a claim that an audience that takes serious offense at particular expression is necessarily likely to disturb the peace, and that the expression may be prohibited on this basis. Our precedents do not countenance such a presumption. On the contrary, they recognize that a principal "function of free speech under our system of government is to invite dispute. It may indeed best serve its high purpose when it induces a condition of unrest, creates dissatisfaction with conditions as they are, or even stirs people to anger." . . .

Thus, we have not permitted the government to assume that every expression of a provocative idea will incite a riot, but have instead required careful consideration of the actual circumstances surrounding such expression, asking whether the expression "is directed to inciting or producing imminent lawless action and is likely to incite or produce such action." . . .

Nor does Johnson's expressive conduct fall within that small class of "fighting words" that are "likely to provoke the average person to retaliation, and thereby cause a breach of the peace." . . . No reasonable onlooker would have regarded Johnson's generalized expression of dissatisfaction with the policies of the federal government as a direct personal insult or an invitation to exchange fisticuffs. . . .

We thus conclude that the state's interest in maintaining order is not implicated on these facts. The state need not worry that our holding will disable it from preserving the peace. We do not suggest that the First Amendment forbids a state to prevent "imminent lawless action." And, in fact, Texas already has a statute specifically prohibiting breaches of the peace . . . which tends to confirm that Texas need not punish this flag desecration in order to keep the peace. . . .

Johnson was prosecuted because he knew that his politically charged expression would cause "serious offense." If he had burned the flag as a means of disposing of it because it was dirty or torn, he would not have been convicted of flag desecration under the Texas law: federal law designates burning as the preferred means of disposing of a flag "when it is in such condition that it is no longer a fitting emblem for display." . . . and Texas has no quarrel with this means of disposal. . . . The Texas law is thus not aimed at protecting the physical integrity of the flag in all circumstances, but is designed instead to protect it only against impairments that would cause serious offense to others. . . .

If there is a bedrock principle underlying the First Amendment, it is that the government may not prohibit the expression of an idea simply because society finds the idea itself offensive or disagreeable. . . . We have not recognized an exception to this principle even where our flag has been involved. In *Street* v. *New York* . . . we held that a state may not criminally punish a person for uttering words critical of the flag. . . .

We never before have held that the Government may insure that a symbol be used to express only one view of that symbol or its referents. . . . To conclude that the Government may permit designated symbols to be used to communicate only a limited set of messages would be to enter territory having no discernible or defensible boundaries. Could the government, on this theory, prohibit the burning of state flags? Of copies of the Presidential seal? Of the Constitution? In evaluating these choices under the First Amendment, how would we decide which symbols were sufficiently special to warrant this unique status? To do so, we would be forced to consult our own political preferences, and impose them on the citizenry, in the very way that the First Amendment forbids us to do.

There is, moreover, no indication—either in the text of the Constitution or in our cases interpreting it—that a separate juridical category exists for the American flag alone. Indeed, we would not be surprised to learn that the persons who framed our Constitution and wrote the amendment that we now construe were not known for their reverence for the Union Jack. . . .

The First Amendment does not guarantee that other concepts virtually sacred to our nation as a whole—such as the principle that discrimination on the basis of race is odious and destructive—will go unquestioned in the marketplace of ideas. We decline, therefore, to create for the flag an exception to the joust of principles protected by the First Amendment. . . .

We are fortified in today's conclusion by our conviction that forbidding criminal punishment for conduct such as Johnson's will not endanger the special role played by our flag or the feelings it inspires. . . . We are tempted to say, in fact, that the flag's deservedly cherished place in our community will be strengthened, not weakened, by our holding today.

Our decision is a reaffirmation of the principles of freedom and inclusiveness that the flag best reflects, and of the conviction that our toleration of criticism such as Johnson's is a sign and source of our strength. Indeed, one of the proudest images of our flag, the one immortalized by our own national anthem, is of the bombardment at Fort McHenry. It is the nation's resilience, not its rigidity, that Texas sees reflected in the flag—and it is that resilience that we assert today.

The way to preserve the flag's special role is not to punish those who feel differently about these matters. It is to persuade them that they are wrong. . . . [P]recisely because it is our flag that is involved, one's response to the flag burner may exploit the uniquely persuasive power of the flag itself. We can imagine no more appropriate response to burning a flag than waving one's own, no better way to counter a flag burner's message than by saluting the flag that burns, no surer means of preserving the dignity even of the flag that burned than by—as one witness here did—according its remains a respectful burial. We do not consecrate the flag by punishing its desecration, for in doing so we dilute the freedom that this cherished emblem represents.

CHIEF JUSTICE REHNQUIST'S
MINORITY DECISION

In writing the minority decision—just one justice's vote short of the majority opinion—Chief Justice Rehnquist used poetry, music and history to support his position. Rehnquist had strong feelings about his point of view, and the gentlemanly chief justice uncharacteristically accused those in the majority of delivering "a regrettably patronizing civics lecture." He wrote:

> In holding this Texas statute unconstitutional, the Court ignores Justice Holmes's familiar aphorism that "a page of history is worth a volume of logic." For more than two hundred years, the American flag has occupied a unique position as the symbol of our nation, a uniqueness that justifies a governmental prohibition against flag burning in the way respondent Johnson did here.
>
> At the time of the American Revolution, the flag served to unify the thirteen colonies at home while obtaining recognition of national sovereignty abroad. Ralph Waldo Emerson's "Concord Hymn" describes

the first skirmishes of the Revolutionary War in these lines:

> *By the rude bridge that arched the flood,*
> *Their flag to April's breeze unfurled,*
> *Here once the embattled farmers stood,*
> *And fired the shot heard round the world. . . .*

During the War of 1812, British forces sailed up Chesapeake Bay and marched overland to sack and burn the city of Washington. They then sailed up the Patapsco River to invest the city of Baltimore, but to do so it was first necessary to reduce Fort McHenry in Baltimore Harbor. Francis Scott Key, a Washington lawyer, had been granted permission by the British to board one of their warships to negotiate the release of an American who had been taken prisoner. That night, waiting anxiously on the British ship, Key watched the British fleet firing on Fort McHenry. Finally, at daybreak, he saw the fort's American flag still flying; the British attack had failed. Intensely moved, he began to scribble on the back of an envelope the poem that became our national anthem. . . . [It was the back of a letter, not an envelope.]

One of the great stories of the Civil War is told in John Greenleaf Whittier's poem "Barbara Frietchie:"

Up from the meadows rich with corn,
Clear in the cool September morn,

The clustered spires of Frederick stand
Green-walled by the hills of Maryland.

Round about them orchards sweep.
Apple- and peach-tree fruited deep,

Fair as the garden of the Lord
To the eyes of the famished rebel horde,

On that pleasant morn of the early fall
When Lee marched over the mountain wall, —

Over the mountains winding down,
Horse and foot, into Frederick town.

Forty flags with their silver stars,
Forty flags with their crimson bars,

Flapped in the morning wind: the sun
Of noon looked down, and saw not one.

Up rose old Barbara Frietchie then,
Bowed with her four-score years and ten;

Bravest of all in Frederick town,
She took up the flag the men hauled down;

In her attic-window the staff she set,
To show that one heart was loyal yet.

Up the street came the rebel tread,
Stonewall Jackson riding ahead.

Under his slouched hat left and right
He glanced: the old flag met his sight.

"Halt!"—the dust-brown ranks stood fast.
"Fire!"—out blazed the rifle-blast

It shivered the window, pane and sash;
It rent the banner with seam and gash.

Quick, as it fell, from the broken staff
Dame Barbara snatched the silken scarf;

She leaned far out on the window-sill,
And shook it forth with a royal will.

"Shoot, if you must, this old gray head,
But spare your country's flag," she said.

A shade of sadness, a blush of shame,
Over the face of the leader came;

The nobler nature within him stirred
To life at that woman's deed and word:

"Who touches a hair of yon gray head
Dies like a dog! March on!" he said.

All day long through Frederick street
Sounded the tread of marching feet:

All day long that free flag tost
Over the heads of the rebel host.

Ever its torn folds rose and fell
On the loyal winds that loved it well;

Perhaps the most famous flag photo ever—the raising of the stars and stripes atop Iwo Jima's Mt. Suribachi, February 23, 1945.

And through the hill-gaps sunset light
Shone over it with a warm good-night.

Barbara Frietchie's work is o'er,
And the Rebel rides on his raids no more.

Honor to her! And let a tear
Fall, for her sake, on Stonewall's bier.

Over Barbara Frietchie's grave,
Flag of Freedom and Union, wave!

Peace and order and beauty draw
Round thy symbol of light and law;

And ever the stars above look down
On thy stars below in Frederick town!

In the First and Second World Wars, thousands of our countrymen died on foreign soil fighting for the American cause. At Iwo Jima in the Second World War, United States Marines fought hand to hand against thousands of Japanese. By the time the marines reached the top of Mount Suribachi, they raised a piece of pipe upright and from one end fluttered a flag. That ascent had cost nearly six thousand American lives. [The photo of this event snapped by Joe Rosenthal became perhaps the most recognizable image of the entire war.] The Iwo Jima Memorial in Arlington National Cemetery memorializes that event. President Franklin Roosevelt authorized the use of the flag on labels, packages, cartons and containers intended for export as lend-lease aid, in order to inform people in other countries of the United States assistance. During the Korean War, the successful amphibious landing of American troops at Inchon was marked by the raising of an American flag within an hour of the event. Impetus for the enactment of the Federal Flag Desecration Statute in 1967 came from the impact of flag burnings in the United States on

179

Police arrest a Chicago man after he set fire to an American flag on the steps of the U.S. Capitol in 1989.

troop morale in Vietnam. Representative L. Mendel Rivers, then Chairman of the House Armed Services Committee, testified that "The burning of the flag . . . has caused my mail to increase one hundred percent from the boys in Vietnam, writing me and asking me what is going on in America." . . .

The flag symbolizes the nation in peace as well as in war. It signifies our national presence on battleships, airplanes, military installations and public buildings from the United States Capitol to the thousands of county courthouses and city halls throughout the country. Two flags are prominently placed in our courtroom. Countless flags are placed by the graves of loved ones each year on what was first called Decoration Day and is now called Memorial Day. . . .

No other American symbol has been as universally honored as the flag. In 1931 Congress declared "The Star-Spangled Banner" to be our national anthem. In 1949 Congress declared June 14 to be Flag Day. In 1987 John Philip Sousa's "The Stars and Stripes Forever" was designated as the national march. Congress has also established "The Pledge of Allegiance to the Flag" and the manner of its deliverance. . . . With the exception of Alaska and Wyoming, all of the states now have statutes prohibiting the burning of the flag. Most of the state statutes are patterned after the Uniform Flag Act of 1917, which . . . provides: "No person shall publicly mutilate, deface, defile, defy, trample upon, or by word or act cast contempt upon any such flag, standard, color, ensign or shield."

The American flag, then, throughout more than two hundred years of our history, has come to be the visible symbol embodying our nation. It does not represent the views of any particular political party, and it does not represent any particular political philosophy. The flag is not simply another "idea" or "point of view" competing for recognition in the marketplace of ideas. Millions and millions of Americans regard it with an almost mystical reverence, regardless of what sort of social, political or philosophical beliefs they may have. I cannot agree that the First Amendment invalidates the Act of Congress, and the laws of forty-eight of the fifty states, which make criminal the public burning of the flag. . . .

The result of the Texas statute is obviously to deny one in Johnson's frame of mind one of many means of "symbolic speech." Far from being a case of "one picture being worth a thousand words," flag burning is the equivalent of an inarticulate grunt or roar that, it seems fair to say, is most likely to be indulged in not to express any particular idea, but to antagonize others. . . .

The Texas statute deprived Johnson of only one rather inarticulate symbolic form of protest—a form of protest that was profoundly offensive to many—and left him with a full panoply of other symbols and every conceivable form of verbal expression to express his deep disapproval of national policy. Thus, in no way can it be said that Texas is punishing him because his hearers—or any other group of people—were profoundly opposed to the message that he sought to convey. Such opposition is no proper basis for restricting speech or expression under the First Amendment. It was Johnson's use of this particular symbol, and not the idea that he sought to convey by it or by his many other expressions, for which he was punished. . . .

But the Court today will have none of this. The uniquely deep awe and respect for our flag felt by virtually all of us are bundled off under the rubric of "designated symbols" that the First Amendment prohibits the government from "establishing." But the Government has not "established" this feeling; two hundred years of history have done that. The government is simply recognizing as a fact the profound regard for the American flag created by that history when it enacts statutes prohibiting the disrespectful public burning of the flag.

The Court concludes its opinion with a regrettably patronizing civics lecture, presumably addressed to the members of both houses of Congress, the members of the forty-eight state legislatures that enacted prohibitions against flag burning, and the troops fighting under that flag in Vietnam who objected to its being burned: "The way to preserve the flag's special role is not to punish those who feel differently about these matters. It is to persuade them that they are wrong."

The Court's role as the final expositor of the Constitution is well established, but its role as a platonic guardian admonishing those responsible to public opinion as if they were truant schoolchildren has no similar place in our system of government. The cry of "no taxation without representation" animated those who revolted against the English Crown to found our nation—the idea that those who submitted to government should have some say as to what kind of laws would be passed. Surely one of the high purposes of a democratic society is to legislate against conduct that is regarded as evil and profoundly offensive to the majority of people—whether it be murder, embezzlement, pollution or flag burning.

Our Constitution wisely places limits on powers of legislative majorities to act, but the declaration of such limits by this Court "is, at all times, a question of much delicacy, which ought seldom, if ever, to be decided in the affirmative, in a doubtful case." Uncritical extension of constitutional protection to the burning of the flag risks the frustration of the very purpose for which organized governments are instituted. The Court decides that the American flag is just another symbol, about which not only must opinions pro and con be tolerated, but for which the most minimal public respect may not be enjoined. The government may conscript men into the armed forces where they must fight and perhaps die for the flag, but the government may not prohibit the public burning of the banner under which they fight. I would uphold the Texas statute as applied in this case.

To overcome the 1989 Supreme Court decision, this following amendment has been introduced in every Congress since then:

SECTION 1.
CONSTITUTIONAL AMENDMENT.

The following article is proposed as an amendment to the Constitution of the United States, which shall be valid to all intents and purposes as part of the Constitution when ratified by the legislatures of three fourths of the several States within seven years after the date of its submission for ratification:

Article —

"The Congress shall have power to prohibit the physical desecration of the flag of the United States."

In the debate on the amendment in the Senate in 2000, Senator Barbara Boxer, Democrat of California, said that she supported a statute that would punish flag burners who want to incite violence, a difficult matter for the courts or the cop on the beat to decide—and the court gets a lot more time to decide what to do than the police officer does—but she opposed changing the Constitution, saying, "The flag stands for freedom, and so does our Bill of Rights. I believe that both must be protected." Since General Colin Powell served as the American military leader during the United States attack on Iraq in the 1991 Gulf War, many people have cited his views on one issue or another. Senator Boxer quoted his position on whether an amendment should be approved to allow laws against flag burning. "I would not amend that great shield of democracy to hammer a few miscreants," General Powell said. "The flag will still be flying proudly long after they have slunk away. Finally, I shudder to think of the legal morass we will create in trying to implement the body of law that will emerge from such an amendment."

Although the amendment attracted support from both parties, the Republican leaders of Congress were its main advocates, so the position of General Powell, a genuine war hero who became secretary of state and a Republican, hurt their chances for victory. Approval of an amendment to the Constitution in the way its advocates were attempting would require passage in both houses of Congress by a two-thirds majority and then approval by the legislatures of three quarters of the states. Approval by the states was a foregone conclusion. Although it had been able to attract an ordinary majority in Congress, the flag desecration amendment had not been able to overcome the two-thirds hurdle. The Republicans even had their own Gulf War hero, General Norman Schwarzkopf, commander of the United States and allied forces there, to support the flag amendment. General Schwarzkopf wrote, in a letter read in the Senate by Orrin Hatch, Republican of Utah, "We are a diverse people living in a complicated, fragmented society. I believe we are imperiled by a growing cynicism [toward] certain traditions that bind us, particularly service to our nation. The flag remains the single preeminent connection to each other and to our country. Legally sanctioning flag desecration only serves to undermine this national unity and identity which must be preserved."

Senator Hatch said during the debate over the amendment:

During the past two days, we have heard several Senators who oppose the flag desecration amendment speak about the American flag as only a symbol or a piece of cloth that should not be confused with the real freedoms that we as Americans enjoy. They want to know why we get so worked up over a symbol, a mere piece of cloth. They want to know why we should care if someone urinates or defecates on the American flag. They ask: Aren't we strong enough as a nation to overlook such behavior?

The U.S. flag is a lot more than a symbol and a lot more than a piece of cloth. Don't take my word for it. Listen to the story of how Mike Christian feels about the American flag. Mike Christian was one of Senator John McCain's cellmates at the "Hanoi Hilton" during the Vietnam war. He sewed an American flag on the inside of his shirt, and he often led his prisoners of war in the Pledge of Allegiance to the flag. One day, his captors found that flag and they beat him severely for possessing it. Despite the risk of even more life-threatening abuse, Mr. Christian sharpened a little piece of bamboo into a needle and painstakingly made another flag out of bits of cloth. His new flag, and the heroics it inspired, helped the other American prisoners survive their prolonged captivity under brutal conditions.

If a makeshift flag can stir such emotions, it is illogical for the Senate to ignore the feelings of the overwhelming number of Americans who support flag protection. The flag is not just a piece of cloth or a symbol. It is the embodiment of our heritage, our liberties, and indeed our sovereignty as a nation. The American flag unites Americans because it embodies shared values and history.

Senator Hatch then traced the history of the flag, beginning with the dubious story of Betsy Ross making the first one on order from George Washington, although he was careful to refer to the tale as a legend, and then went on.

I fear that the significance of these flags, and their meaning to Americans, is being belittled by some who suggest the Senate's time is too important for the flag protection constitutional amendment.

Listen to the American people. That is what I would like to say to the Members of the Senate. The vast majority of our citizens support amending the Constitution to protect our nation's flag. To us, protecting the flag as the symbol of our national community—and utilizing the constitutional amendment process to do so—is no trivial matter.

There are tens of thousands of veterans living in our country today who have put their lives on the line to defend our flag and the principles for which it stands. Those are the fortunate ones who were not required to make the ultimate sacrifice, as did my brother and my brother-in-law. For every one of those, there is someone who has traded the life of a loved one for a flag, folded at a funeral. Let's think about that trade—and about the people who made that sacrifice for us—before deciding whether the flag is important enough to be addressed in the Senate.

Would it really trivialize the Constitution, as some critics suggest, to pass an amendment that is supported by a vast majority of Americans? Is it somehow frivolous to employ the amendment process that our Founding Fathers wrote into Article V of the Constitution? Are we irresponsible if we simply restore the law as it existed for centuries prior to two recent Supreme Court decisions?

The Constitution itself establishes the process for its own amendment. It says that the Constitution will be amended when two thirds of Congress and three fourths of the states want to do so. It does not say that this procedure is reserved for issues that some law professors think are important, or for an issue that would immediately crush the foundations of our great republic if left unaddressed. If "government by the people" means anything, it means that the people can decide the fundamental questions concerning the checks and balances in our government. It means the people can choose whether it is Congress or the Supreme Court that decides whether flag desecration is against the law. The people have said that they want Congress to decide it in the state legislatures.

I urge my colleagues to think hard about what they consider "important" before they conclude that the Senate should ignore the people's desire to make decisions about the government which governs them. The flag amendment is the very essence of "government by the people" because it reflects the people's decision to give Congress a power that the Supreme Court has taken away. This question is very important. It involves the separation-of-power doctrine of our Constitution.

As he spoke during the debate in 2000, Senator Hatch knew that his side did not have the votes for the required two-thirds approval. In 1995 and 1997, the House of Representatives approved the constitutional amendment by more than the two-thirds majority. It did so again in 1999, by a vote of three hundred five to one hundred twenty-four, well above the required mark, and that was what was before the Senate in 2000. Hatch was a good vote counter, as usual, and the Senate voted sixty-three to thirty-seven in favor of sending the amendment to the states for approval, a majority, but four votes below the two thirds needed. Voting for the amendment were fifty-one Republicans and twelve Democrats, and voting against it were thirty-three Democrats and four Republicans. It was the fourth time that the Senate had failed to muster the two-thirds majority for the amendment.

In the debate in the House, Representative Randy (Duke) Cunningham, Republican of California, said, "I ask members to give themselves a vision: Iwo Jima, and the men that put up that American flag. Now allow some hippie to go up there and burn it."

Representative John Conyers, Jr., Democrat of Michigan, said that flag burning was not a problem that called for fixing with a constitutional amendment, maintaining that only seventy-two cases had been reported in the nineteen nineties.

Representative Melvin L. Watt, Democrat of North Carolina, said, "I abhor flag burners," but he added, "I am here to defend the First Amendment. I am here to defend the freedom of expression. I am here to defend the right of people who have views that are contrary to mine to express those views."

Two hundred ten Republicans and ninety-five Democrats voted for the constitutional amendment, while one hundred thirteen Democrats, ten Republicans and one independent voted against it.

Senator Jon Kyl, Republican of Arizona, told the Senate, "I cannot believe that our Founding Fathers intended 'freedom of expression' to encompass the willful destruction of our national symbol—the symbol of America that so many of our sons and daughters have given their lives to defend."

Senator Russell D. Feingold, Democrat of Wisconsin, responded to Senator Kyl by saying:

I daresay that there is not a Senator among us who does not feel goose bumps when first looking up at the dome of the Capitol and seeing our flag. I would wager that no U.S. Senator fails to get a lump in the throat when standing to the strains of the national anthem. And I am confident that there is none among us whose eyes do not sometimes mist over when watching those seven bars of red and six of white ripple in the breeze and tug at the heart.

But, my colleagues, honoring the flag demands that we here fully and fairly debate this amendment. Amending the Constitution is an undertaking of the greatest import. . . . Honor demands that we view any effort to amend the Constitution with trepidation. Since the adoption of the Bill of Rights in 1791, America has amended its Constitution on only seventeen occasions. Our Constitution has served this nation well and withstood the test of time, in large part because Congress has resisted the urge to respond to every adversity, real or imagined, with a constitutional amendment. We should exercise restraint in amending this great charter.

We honor the American flag because we love "the Republic for which it stands." We honor the banner because we cherish "one nation . . . with liberty and justice for all." We honor the flag because it represents a Constitution, that solemn commitment; and a Bill of Rights, that charter of liberty; unrivaled in the history of humankind.

Honor demands that we seek to protect not just the flag, but the principles in that Constitution and that Bill of Rights—principles of freedom, opportunity, and liberty. I believe these principles, as much as our nation's cherished symbols, frame our history and define our nation. As dearly as we hold the flag, we must hold these principles at least as dearly.

Yes, there have been some handfuls of sociopaths who burn our flag to thrust a firebrand in our eye. The question before us today is: Will the misguided actions of these few misfits cause us to curtail our fundamental principles of freedom? We would only grant them victory if we allow their despicable acts to goad us into desecrating the greatest protection of individual rights in human history—our Bill of Rights. As Senator Bob Kerrey has said: "Patriotism calls upon us to be brave enough to endure and withstand such an act—to tolerate the intolerable."

Let us show our strength, by not rising to the bait. Let us show our bravery, by not giving the flag burners what they want. Let us show our faith in the strength of this country and its institutions, by not lashing out in anger at those who would defile our flag. The costs of this amendment would exact far too great a price to pay. This amendment, if adopted, would criminalize the very acts that the Supreme Court has held to be protected by the First Amendment. This amendment would clearly and intentionally erode the Bill of Rights.

This amendment would have an unprecedented, direct, and adverse effect on the freedoms embodied in the Bill of Rights. For the first time in our history, this amendment would employ the Constitution and the Bill of Rights—both premised on the idea of limiting the Government—to limit individual rights, and, in particular, the freedom of speech. Our former colleague, Senator John Glenn, said it very well last year. He said: "Our revered symbol stands for freedom, but is not freedom itself. We must not let those who revile our way of

life trick us into diminishing our great gift or even
take a chance of diminishing our freedoms."

Senator Feingold raised the question of what to do
with the incidental uses of the flag. In many countries, the
flag has been adapted as clothing. Not long ago there was
a widely published photograph of Prince William, heir to
the British throne, wearing a vest in the design of a Union
Jack. Would a jacket made in the style of the Stars and
Stripes run afoul of the law? Would it make any differ-
ence if the wearer was dressed up as a patriotic Uncle Sam
or as a punk rocker using a flag design as a patch covering
a spot on the buttocks? And is there any greater desecration of the flag than as to use it for commercial purposes?
Large flags are displayed in front of used car dealerships
on commercial highways all over the country.

Feingold asked:

How would the amendment affect flags on
T-shirts? How would the amendment affect flags
on scarves? In the memorable example given by the
late and revered Senator John Chafee last year, how
would the amendment affect a handmade flag rug?
Now the amendment, of course, does not make anything illegal by itself. It simply gives the Congress the
power to prohibit the physical desecration of
the flag. But the question is still a powerful one. We
must still ask: What kind of statute would this
amendment insulate from constitutional attack?

Would this amendment permit Congress to enact a statute that would criminalize wearing a T-shirt with a flag on it? Or could Congress criminalize tearing such a T-shirt? Would the amendment permit Congress to criminalize wearing a scarf with a flag on it? Or could Congress criminalize spitting on such a scarf? Would this amendment permit Congress to criminalize making a rug with a flag on it? Or could Congress criminalize stepping on such a rug?

As often happens in such debates, Senator Paul Wellstone, Democrat of Minnesota, introduced his personal history in making his point:

My father was a Jewish immigrant born in the Ukraine and who fled persecution from Russia. My mother's family came from the Ukraine as well. As a first generation American on my father's side, I revere the flag and I am fiercely patriotic. I love to see the flag flying over the Capitol. I love to recite the Pledge of Allegiance to the flag. I think it is a beautiful, powerful symbol of American democracy. What I learned from my parents more than anything else, and from my own family experience as the son of a Jewish immigrant who fled czarist Russia, is that my father came to the United States because of the freedom—the freedom we have as American citizens to express our views openly, without fear of punishment. I am deeply impressed with the sincerity of those who, including Senator Hatch, favor this constitutional amendment. I am impressed with the sacrifice and patriotism of those veterans who support this constitutional amendment. I think in the veterans community there certainly are differences of opinion. I do not question their sincerity or commitment at all.

It is with a great deal of respect for those with whom I disagree, including some members of the American Legion, that I oppose this amendment. I oppose it because, to me, it is ultimately the freedom that matters the most. To me, the soul of the flag, as opposed to the physical part of the flag, is the freedom that it stands for, the freedom that my parents talked about with me, the freedom that all of us have to speak up. I do not want to amend the Bill of Rights for the first time in its 209 years of existence. I don't want to amend the First Amendment, the founding principle of freedom of speech from which all other freedoms follow.

Senator Wellstone also invoked the memory of Senator John Chafee, the Rhode Island Republican, in opposing the flag desecration amendment, saying, "Our late and dear friend and colleague, Senator John Chafee, who was a highly decorated soldier in two wars, wrote: 'We cannot mandate respect and pride in the flag. In fact, in my view, taking steps to require citizens to respect the flag sullies its significance and its symbolism.' "

Senator Edward M. Kennedy, Democrat of Massachusetts, said:

Flag burning is a vile and contemptuous act, but it is also a form of expression protected by the First Amendment. Surely we are not so insecure in our commitment to freedom of speech and the First Amendment that we are willing to start carving loopholes now in that majestic language. I strongly oppose the constitutional amendment we are debating today. The First Amendment is one of the great pillars of our freedom and democracy. It has never been amended in over two hundred years of our history, and now is no time to start. There is not even a plausible factual basis for carving a hole in the heart of the First Amendment. There is no significant problem. Flag burning is exceedingly rare. Published reports indicate that fewer than ten flag burning incidents have occurred a year since the Supreme Court's decision in *Texas* v. *Johnson* in 1989 on the First Amendment. Over the last five years, there was only one such incident in Massachusetts. This is hardly the kind of serious and widespread problem in American life that warrants an assault on the First Amendment. Surely there is no clear and present danger that warrants such a change. This proposal fails the reality test. The

Constitution is not a billboard on which to plaster amendments as if they were bumper sticker slogans. . . .

I remember listening to a speech given by Justice Douglas, one of the great Supreme Court Justices of this century. Students asked him: What was the most important export of the United States? He said, without hesitation: The First Amendment because it is the defining amendment for the preservation of free speech as the basic and fundamental right in shaping our nation. Clearly, it would be a mistake of historic proportions for this Congress to make the first alteration to the First Amendment in more than two centuries. The First Amendment breathes light into the very concept of our democracy. It protects the freedoms of all Americans, including the fundamental freedom of citizens to criticize their government and the country itself, including the flag. . . . The flag is a symbol that embodies all that is great and good about America. It symbolizes our patriotism, our achievements and, above all, our respect for our freedoms and our democracy. We do not honor the flag by dishonoring the First Amendment.

Senator Hatch took offense at the suggestion that those who supported the flag desecration amendment were dishonoring the First Amendment, "that we are somehow

Neanderthals, the eighty percent of the people in this country who want to protect our national symbol from acts of physical desecration."

"The funny thing about it," he went on, "this amendment does not even do that. All this amendment does is restore the power of the Congress to be able to pass a statute if the Congress so chooses, something that we have to do by constitutional amendment if we want to be coequal with the judicial branch of government."

Senator Rod Grams, Republican of Minnesota, advocated the constitutional amendment with a bit of lawyer bashing, which is never out of favor in Congress, although it is a body in which lawyers are not exactly an oppressed minority. "The Constitution begins with the ringing words *We the People* for a reason," Grams said. "In our great nation, the people are empowered to decide the manner in which we are to be governed and the values we are to uphold. I join eighty percent of the American people in the belief the flag of the United States of America should be protected from physical desecration. And I am blessed to live in a nation where the will of the people can triumph over that of lawyers and judges."

Because of the Supreme Court decision, Senator Grams said, "a constitutional amendment is clearly necessary to protect our flag." The campaign to win approval of the amendment, he said, "is a fight to restore duty, honor, and love of country to their rightful place."

Senator Grams told the Senate:

Sadly, patriotism is on the decline. That's dangerous in a democracy. Just ask the military recruiters who can't find enough willing young people to fill the ranks of our military during this strong economy. What happened to the pride in serving your country? Where are the Americans willing to answer the call?

Protecting the flag reflects our desire to protect our nation from this erosion in patriotism. It signals that our government, as a reflection of the will of the people, believes all Americans should treat the flag with respect. The men and women of our armed forces who sacrificed for the flag should be shown they did not do so in vain. They fought, suffered, and died to preserve the very freedom and liberty which allow us to proclaim that desecrating the American flag goes too far and should be prohibited. To say that our flag is just a piece of cloth — a rag that can be defiled and trampled upon and even burnt into ashes — is to dishonor every soldier who ever fought to protect it. Every star, every stripe, on our flag was bought through their sacrifice.

The flag of the United States of America is a true national treasure. Because of all that it symbolizes, we have always held our flag with the greatest esteem, with reverence. That is why we fly it so high above us. When the flag is aloft, it stands above political division and above partisanship. Under our flag, we are united. Most Americans cannot understand why anyone would burn a flag. Most Americans cannot understand why the Senate would not act decisively and overwhelmingly to pass an amendment affording our flag the protection it deserves.

This simple piece of cloth is indeed worthy of constitutional protection. I urge my colleagues to follow the will of "We the People" and accord the American flag the dignity it is due.

Senator Hatch offered this view of American history:

Opponents of the constitutional amendment argue that this would be an unprecedented infringement on the freedom of speech, which does not satisfy James Madison's counsel that amendments of the Constitution should be limited to "certain great and extraordinary circumstances." Setting aside the fact that flag desecration is conduct, not speech, and that our freedom of speech is not absolute, these critics never fully address the fact that our Founding Fathers, James Madison in particular, saw protection of the flag as falling outside the scope of the First Amendment and was more a matter of protecting national sovereignty. The original intent of the nation's founders indicates the importance of protecting the flag as a symbol of American sovereignty. Madison and Jefferson consistently emphasized the legal significance of infractions on the physical integrity of the flag.

For example, one of Madison's earliest pronouncements concerned an incident in October 1800 when an Algerian ship forced a U.S. Man of War—the *George Washington*—to haul down its flag and replace it with the flag from Algiers. As secretary of state under Thomas Jefferson, Madison pronounced such a situation as a matter of international law, a dire invasion of sovereignty which "on a fit occasion" might be "revised." Madison continued his defense of the integrity of the flag when he pronounced an active flag defacement in the streets of an American city to be a violation of law. On June 22, 1807, when a British ship fired upon and ordered the lowering of an American frigate's flag, Madison told the British ambassador "that the attack . . . was a detached, flagrant insult to the flag and sovereignty of the United States." Madison believed that "the indignity offered to the sovereignty and flag of the nation demands . . . an honorable reparation." Madison's statements suggest his belief that protecting the physical integrity of the flag ensured the protections of the nation's sovereignty. This is the author of the Constitution. . . .

Madison did not conclude, as some defenders of the right to deface the flag contend, that the First Amendment protected the rights of Americans to tear down a flag or that defacing the flag was a form of expression protected by the First Amendment. On the contrary. It would appear that Madison had an intimate familiarity with the significance of protecting the physical integrity of the flag, especially as such protection related to the First Amendment, which he helped draft and move through the First Congress. He knew there had been no intent to withdraw the traditional physical protection from the flag. Madison and Jefferson intended for the Government to be able to protect the flag consistent with the Bill of Rights. This was based on their belief that obtaining sovereign treatment was distinct from an interest in protecting against the suppression of expression. Madison and Jefferson consistently demonstrated that they sought commerce, citizenship and neutrality rights through the protection of the flag. They did not seek to suppress the expression of alternative "ideas," "messages," "views," or "meanings."

Senator Hatch told his colleagues: "We took this flag . . . and planted it for eternity on the moon. We carry it into battle. We salute it and pledge allegiance to it. Men and women have died for it and have been tortured for their fidelity to it. As Americans we recognize and believe that the flag is our unique symbol of unity and sovereignty. As Madison noted, the flag is a unique incident which, when desecrated, 'demands an honorable reparation.' "

11

Saving America's Most Famous Flag for Our Grandchildren

In 1996, when the Star-Spangled Banner was 183 years old, the Smithsonian Institution began a conservation project on the flag and concluded in 2000 that, although the flag was in extremely fragile condition, it could last an additional five hundred to a thousand years under public display in which light, humidity and temperature are carefully controlled. The project will cost $18 million for the conservation work, a new display for the flag, an endowment for its future care, public and educational programs and other things. The conservation project was designed to be a painstaking one and, in keeping with the national significance of the object being conserved, was done in full view of the public, with the Smithsonian's National

Museum of American History setting up a laboratory with glass walls fifty feet high so that visitors to the museum could watch what was going on.

First the flag was carefully taken from the wall where it had been displayed, vacuumed lightly and rolled onto a tube thirty-two feet long and two feet wide that looked like a huge paper towel holder. The tube was then slowly moved to the laboratory and the flag, with its linen backing still attached, was carefully unrolled, inch by inch, onto a gigantic aluminum table as workers on a gantry—sort of a rolling bridge—lay on their stomachs or sides and knelt four or five inches above it to snip off the 1.7 million threads holding it to the linen backing, most while the flag was still on the roller. On a good day, one worker could remove the stitches from one to three square feet of the flag, but the work was so tiring that frequent rest breaks were needed. Anthony Maher, a project manager for the architectural and engineering firm of KCF-SHG, which designed the facility, said, "There was no precedent for a project like this, so you learn as you go." When that phase of the project was finished, the flag was seen without the linen stitches for the first time since they were sewn on to hold the linen backing in 1914. The conservators were pleased to find that the colors were brighter and much more vibrant than they had appeared before. When the web of stitches was removed, the faded linen threads disappeared. In addition, a quilting effect had been created where the threads held the flag to the backing, and that effect is expected to disappear over time. Fibers had been damaged by this quilting effect, so the removal of the stitches eliminated that danger while making the flag appear more brilliant.

Many historians, not aware of or in accord with current thinking that leans toward a different flag—the storm flag—flying during the battle, had thought that the Star-Spangled Banner had eleven patches covering holes caused by the British shelling in 1814. Lonn Taylor, the Smithsonian historian who has studied the Star-Spangled Banner, feels that the jury is still out on the question of what flag flew during the battle and that it may indeed have been flying then and was damaged by British shot. Conservationists have found that twenty-seven areas had been patched over during the flag's long life and the cause of the holes is still uncertain. In some areas, the damage from fabric loss and deterioration was greater than had been thought, with some stripes having lost more than sixty percent of their original material. Some frayed pieces had become detached, held in place only by the linen backing they were sewn to, so one problem was to find a way to preserve the loose pieces in place. Stains that appear to be from ink and resemble cursive writing were found, suggesting that someone had signed the flag at some point, perhaps Major George Armistead, the commander of Fort McHenry.

After all the linen stitches were snipped, the conservators placed a temporary lightweight cover over the flag.

The cover, called a marquisette, was made of an open-weave polyester and was similar to a wedding veil. The purpose of the cover was to protect the loosened flag as it was rerolled onto the tube, then unrolled, this time with the linen backing on the top. The next step was to gently remove the linen backing, examine the "hidden" side for the first time since 1873—except for the six-week period when the canvas backing was removed in 1914 until the linen was attached—and decide how to go about the cleaning. The Smithsonian hopes to have the flag fully conserved and on display by 2002. "This exhibition will place the Star-Spangled Banner in a historic and cultural context, tracing its transformation from a battle relic into a treasured national icon," said Spencer R. Crew, director of the National Museum of American History. "It will connect this banner to the larger story of the American flag in American life."

While everyone stressed the place of the Star-Spangled Banner as a symbol of America, much of the research into its wool content came from studies in Australia and New Zealand, not the United States. "New Zealand and Australia have traditionally had stronger research programs," said Suzanne Thomassen-Krauss, the Smithsonian's senior textile conservator for the project. Research on the flag was conducted on the conservation site by New Zealand experts working with American specialists.

The flag once had a huge protective cover that was raised every hour on the hour, to reveal the flag behind it, to the accompaniment of "The Star-Spangled Banner," but the cover broke in 1994. When that happened, said Ronald E. Becker, the Smithsonian official responsible for the cleaning project, "We saw it as an opportunity to not just replace it but to renew our conservation efforts to study the flag today."

12

What the Future Holds for the National Anthem

In the debate in the Senate over the proposed constitutional amendment designed to permit laws against flag desecration, Senator Robert C. Byrd, the West Virginia Democrat and the Senate's leading authority on the Constitution, changed his old position of favoring the amendment to one of opposition. One of his reasons for changing his mind was a reflection on the failure of the Eighteenth Amendment, which instituted Prohibition and was, as he said, "routinely ignored and violated" until it was repealed by the Twenty-first Amendment.

"Prohibition not only made criminals and scofflaws of countless Americans," he said, "it also placed them in violation of the Constitution. I can remember the revenue officers, when they came to the coal camps and when they scoured around the hills and the mountains looking for the moonshine stills. I can remember the Revenuers. That was a terrible mistake, and, while the blemish to the Constitution has since faded, the lesson may not have been learned. Thus, a constitutional amendment against flag burning may very well prove to be counterproductive, just as did the Prohibition amendment. If this were to happen, our Constitution would be diminished and flag burning would continue."

Senator Daniel Patrick Moynihan, Democrat of New York, opposed the amendment, saying, "Surely, there would be no one, however unintentionally—and I say this as a member of the American Legion—who would propose that to debase the First Amendment to the Constitution meets the criteria of upholding and defending it." He urged the senators to "walk away from this trivializing of our most sacred trust. Defeat this amendment."

Byrd's comments, which he made in a Senate speech, show how much thoughtful study he has given to the Constitution and to American society, and in another section, in an almost offhand remark, he said, "Key's words are so familiar that we may scarcely think of them when we hear or sing them." Byrd was right. Through endless repetition, the national anthem has lost its impact.

Paul Zimmerman, the *Sports Illustrated* writer who is so bored by the anthem that he times its performance, hoping to get it over with quickly, is not alone is suggesting that some other song be adopted, and "America the Beautiful" gets the most support as an alternative. A few years ago, three members of the House of Representatives had introduced bills that would have changed things. Representative Andrew Jacobs, Jr., Democrat of Indiana, wanted "America the Beautiful" to be declared the national anthem. Representative E. (Kika) de la Garza, Democrat of Texas, also wanted "America the Beautiful" to be declared the national *song*. Representative James H. Quillen, Republican of Tennessee, wanted "Stars and Stripes Forever" to be declared the national *march*. When I asked Jacobs about the prospects for his bill, he was optimistic and said, "It's going to pass—around the turn of the century." The century has turned. Jacobs is gone. De la Garza is gone. Quillen is gone. "The Star-Spangled Banner" is still here. Jacobs's bill hasn't passed. It won't ever pass.

Jacobs based most of his objections on "The Star-Spangled Banner's" past as an English drinking song and on the fact that it is based on a battle, arguments that were heard and rejected before Congress passed its legislation adopting our national anthem in 1931. In "America the Beautiful's" favor, Jacobs said, were that it was home-grown and is "not about an American battle and not about the American flag, but about the American people."

"God Bless America" gets a lot of support, but that seems to have peaked when Kate Smith was adopted as a sort of mascot by the Philadelphia Flyers hockey team, which won more games when that classic by Irving Berlin was played in place of "The Star-Spangled Banner." Since most of the players on the team were from Canada, it is hard to imagine them drawing inspiration from either song. Antiestablishment types might suggest "This Land Is Your Land," which Woodie Guthrie wrote as an antidote to "God Bless America," as he found it too saccharine. In fact, the leftist Guthrie's original title for his song was "God Blessed America," which he wisely changed to his loving and certainly more original title. While "God Bless America" will always have its mainstream admirers, it will never overtake "The Star-Spangled Banner" as our national anthem. Similarly, "This Land Is Your Land" will always have a fond following, especially among the young and among devotees of folk music, but it, too, will always be an also-ran in these sweepstakes.

Where does all this leave us? We've got a Grand Old Flag, as George M. Cohan wrote. Long may it wave. We've got a barely singable national anthem based on it that many people would like to get rid of. It's not going to happen. What Francis Scott Key started that night in 1814 in Baltimore Harbor will be with us forever in the land of the free.

New York City firemen raise the Stars and Stripes atop the rubble of the World Trade Center on the afternoon of September 11, 2001. It is eerily reminiscent of the famous photo of the flag raising on Iwo Jima during World War II.

Epilogue

September 11, 2001

All Americans will remember where they were on September 11, 2001, when the United States was hit by terrorist attacks at the World Trade Center in New York City and the Pentagon in Washington, D.C., just as members of an earlier generation remembered where they were on December 7, 1941, when the Japanese attacked Pearl Harbor. In 2001, as in 1941, Americans rallied round their flag with an outpouring of patriotism that reflected the outrage and sorrow that we felt. In many cases, it took the form of flying the Star-Spangled Banner. In fact, so many American flags were bought by so many people who never would have even thought of flying them that Wal-Mart, the nation's largest retailer, ran out of flags.

In 2000, Wal-Mart sold just 26,000 American flags in

the entire month of September. In 2001, before exhausting its stocks, it sold 450,000 in the three days beginning with September 11, and just about every retailer in the United States, big and small, ran out of flags to sell. Wal-Mart ordered more from its suppliers and resumed selling the flags, ranging from $1.97 for a kit of four four- by six-inch flags to $24.97 for single flags measuring four by six feet. Some were made of cotton, which Mary Pickersgill would have been familiar with, the cheaper ones of nylon or a polyester-cotton blend. Pickersgill would have been baffled by those. A month after the attacks, Wal-Mart was still selling lots of flags. "They're flying off the shelves," Sharon Weber, a Wal-Mart spokeswoman, said at the company's headquarters in Bentonville, Arkansas, enjoying the figure of speech. Instead of devoting a portion of the sales of the flags to the relief efforts, Wal-Mart did even more, raising $14 million in cash and merchandise from its customers and sales staff in less than a month. The merchandise was sent to fill the requests of the American Red Cross and the Salvation Army, whose staff and volunteers needed things like bottled water, rubbing alcohol, dog food and dog booties. The dog food, of course, was for the rescue dogs that were being used to hunt for possible survivors buried in the rubble of the World Trade Center. But booties? "They were shoes for dogs because the ground was so hot," Weber said. "We sent whatever the American Red Cross said they needed." When asked whether Wal-Mart's flags were domestic or imported, she answered, "We only sell flags that are made in the United States." That is a widespread attitude among large retailers, but many flags sold in the United States are made in China and Taiwan, with the foreign-made flags selling for less than American ones.

One of Wal-Mart's major suppliers is Annin & Company, of Roseland, New Jersey, which normally made 30,000 flags a week. Annin pushed its production up to 100,000 a week and still could not meet the demand. It was able to increase production of the Star-Spangled Banner by shifting some workers from their normal tasks of making nautical, golf course, state and foreign flags. Another manufacturer, Valley Forge Flag, of Womelsdorf, Pennsylvania, increased production of its three- by five-foot flags from 10,000 a week to 40,000. At the National Flag and Display Company, on the East Side of Manhattan, just a few miles from the World Trade Center, the stock was quickly sold out.

During a normal September, Freedom Flag and Banner, in Miami, would expect to sell 25 flags. In September 2001, it sold more than 200,000. Barbara Dabney, Freedom's owner, said that the company sold its cheaper flags, which have the stars and stripes printed on the fabric, for $10 to $15, with the nylon versions costing more than those made of polyester. The flags are three by five feet, and the versions made with embroidered stars and the stripes sewn in individually cost $35 for the same size. "The flag companies have always been a barometer of what's going on in the country," Dabney said. While her flags are made in the United States, the people who make them were not born here. "Haiti, Cuba, Nicaragua," Dabney ticked off as she remembered where her workers were from. "Trinidad, Ecuador." In fact, the only native-born Americans in her factory were from Puerto Rico. Some of Freedom's flags are made elsewhere and shipped to Miami for resale, and Dabney always gets a thrill when she opens a package with finely embroidered American flags. "It takes your breath away," she said.

Many newspapers published images of American flags so that people who could not get to stores fast enough to buy the real thing were able to put printed images in their windows. Flags sprung up everywhere—from the front porches of suburban homes, from windows of apartment houses, on the sides of office buildings, stores and factories, on car antennas, on fire engines, on the shirts of athletes, on the caps of every major league baseball player, even small ones stuck onto the badges police officers have on their hats. Before September 11, New York City, the hardest hit of the terrorist targets, probably would have been considered the least likely place in the United States to have waved the flag, but wave it they did. This is not to suggest that New Yorkers are not as patriotic as anyone else, but rather that Manhattanites (those who represent New York to the rest of the country and the world, a mind-set that tends to ignore Queens, Brooklyn, the Bronx and Staten Island) might regard an outright display of patriotism as just plain uncool. After the attacks, everyone seemed to wear a flag pin or fly a flag from a home or a car. Madonna wore a kilt with a flag design during a performance in Los Angeles, and the British rock star P J Harvey wore red, white and blue boots during an appearance on *The Tonight Show*. They weren't the only ones. Manufacturers quickly distributed clothing bearing the flag of the United States.

A friend of mine, who lives in Greenwich Village, not far from the World Trade Center, was indescribably shocked by the terrorist attack and by the deaths of the firemen and police officers who rushed into the stricken buildings in an attempt to save others. "I've got flags in a bunch of places—on the car window, on one of the apartment windows, in the lapels of jackets," said this sophisticated New Yorker, who is in the publishing business. "It's not my usual thing. I'm very patriotic—hey, I've lived elsewhere and I know what it can be like—but not in the usual flag-waving way. But the World Trade Center attack has been so searing in so many ways, and we don't even know anyone personally who was involved, although one of our local firehouses lost ten men. I can't pass it without dropping money or leaving a flower."

Why the flags? "They give me a sense of telling the victims that I care about their pain, that I actually feel it," my friend said. "It's also showing support for this country, which I love and which I feel is in a terrible crisis. I want to—I need to—show that I'm part of the effort to stop all of it. If America can't crush these guys, no one can."

Many of the dry cleaners, groceries and other stores in New York are run by immigrants and many—perhaps a majority—of the taxis are driven by immigrants, and they especially flew the flags, as if to say, "I am an American." Many of those immigrants are from the Middle East and Central Asia, which is also where the terrorists came from, and these new Americans felt that it was important to show their new loyalty to the Stars and Stripes.

It's a free country, of course, so the wretched excess, commercialism and bad taste that accompanied the genuine outpourings of grief had to be accepted. In the window of a shop in downtown Washington, I saw mannequins dressed in bikinis whose material depicted the American flag (would the proposed flag desecration amendment apply to bad taste?), and a commercial on television offered, at a high price, sets of small flags that, if you looked close enough, turned out to be cheap plastic. There were T-shirts with the flag alone and T-shirts with the flags and the buildings of the World Trade Center. In New York, sidewalk hawkers quickly sold supplies of flag-imprinted T-shirts that proclaimed: "I Survived the Attacks." On the other hand, Old Navy dedicated all of its profits for disaster relief from the sales of T-shirts showing the flag above the printed legend United States of America.

The move to gain passage of the flag-burning amendment to the Constitution got just a slight boost from the outburst of patriotism. Ed Bergassi, a New York businessman, said, "The desecration of the American flag should not be tolerated. We must get the message through to the Senate." Senator Charles Schumer, a New York Democrat, replied that the Constitution should not be changed just because a small number of people burned the flag.

"The answer to flag burning is flag waving," Senator Schumer said.

My family and I were in Italy when the terrorists struck, and several people in our small village who knew we were Americans came up to us to express their sympathy. The road that leads down the hill from the village to the main road is not wide enough for two cars to pass each other, so when a car going downhill comes across another going up, they each have to slow down and squeeze over to the right side of the road. Once a driver stopped as we passed each other. She rolled down her window and said, "I'm so sorry." We saw posters throughout Tuscany expressing condolences to the United States, and many shops in places like Florence, Siena and Cortona had tiny American flags in their windows and expressions of sympathy taped to their doors. Some newspaper images of the flag stay in my mind. In *l'Unita*, the newspaper of the former Communist Party in Italy, which was sympathetic to the United States in its coverage of the attack (as was the party itself), ran a front-page picture that showed supporters of Osama bin Laden stomping on an American flag. A copy of the *Washington Post* that was brought to me in Italy by a visiting niece showed members of the Colorado Rockies and Arizona Diamondbacks baseball teams holding a huge American flag that covered half of the infield before their game that marked the resumption of play. We got most of our news about the attacks from the *International Herald Tribune*, the Paris-based newspaper where I had worked during the summer, and from radio reports on the shortwave service of the British Broadcasting Corporation, which dropped virtually all of its normal programs to cover the terrorism. So my family was fairly well informed, but no news reports could adequately convey the horror that our friends in New York and Washington had gone through. It was almost a month after the attack that we saw for ourselves something of what the country had experienced—when we drove past the Pentagon and saw the huge gash in one side and the smoke-blackened walls of the surviving section.

The terrorist attacks were especially trying for Americans of Muslim background, particularly Arabs. Just a few days after the horror, Yasir El-Maghrbi, who is from Libya, took the oath as an American citizen along with 37 others at the United States District Court in Washington, and said that he was ready to take up arms to defend his new country if called upon. He told the *Washington Post,* "I'll fight whatever fight against people who want to destroy the system we have in the United States." Another new citizen, Zaheer Ahmad Bajwa, who is from Pakistan, was concerned that he might be discriminated against because of his Islamic background, which did happen to others in the days immediately following the attacks. He told the *Post,* "I came here because I love this country. If I have to prove my ID everywhere, it's not the same United States of America." Perhaps it was understandable that innocent Muslims came under suspicion, but it was a misplaced sentiment. Hundreds of American Muslims worked in the World Trade Center. Hundreds of them died there.

The terrorist attacks of September 11 brought on renewed popularity for the American national anthem. A British military band, the Coldstream Guards, for example, played "The Star-Spangled Banner" at the Changing of the Guard ceremony at Buckingham Palace in London on September 13, two days after the attacks. The unprecedented tribute to the fallen Americans was ordered by Queen Elizabeth II, and her son Prince Andrew was on hand for the ceremony, accompanied by the American ambassador to Britain, William Farish. Thousands of American and other foreign tourists, as well as British citizens, held American flags, and many wept. At first, the crowd listened in silence to the band and then, slowly, many started singing "The Star-Spangled Banner" through their tears, holding their hands over their hearts. And then the crowd observed two minutes of silence. One American tourist, Laura Esposito, of Boston, who wore a jacket with the Stars and Stripes pattern, told the British newspaper the *Guardian*, "I want to be closer to home right now, and this is the closest we can get." Jenny Lee, a visitor from San Francisco, held a cardboard American flag that she had made and told the *Telegraph*, "I was really touched that the queen has done this. Even though I'm so many miles from home, I feel that Britain is really with us on this one." Among the grateful Americans who were deeply moved by the Coldstream Guards' rendition of the national anthem, which was broadcast on United States television, was Mayor Rudolph Giuliani of New York, who invited the band to perform in New York. The queen attended a special remembrance service the next day at St. Paul's Cathedral. In the City, London's financial center, the Lloyd's of London insurance group rang the old Lutine Bell, following a tradition that was used to announce a disaster at sea and now used only for special occasions.

In Paris on the day of mourning, all of the television screens in the big Virgin store on the Champs-Elysées showed the American flag at half-staff as customers and salespeople stood in silence. The British paper the *Independent* reported this scene: At Edinburgh Castle in Scotland, workers who were dismantling scaffolding raised an American flag on the structure, and it became the focal point of silence in that busy area, a silence that was broken only by a man who began singing "The Star-Spangled Banner," an event that brought tears to the eyes of the many people who witnessed it. In England, in the rural village of Dunham Massey, someone pinned a card in the post office window that said "God Bless America," accompanied by a small American flag.

Many people use familiar tunes that play when their cellphones ring, but "The Star-Spangled Banner" had been used by very few people before September 11. After the terrorist attack, AT&T Wireless reported that the national anthem leapt more than 400 places to become the No. 1 tune by September 13. It was followed by "America the Beautiful" at No. 2 and "God Bless America" at No. 4. No. 3 was "Follow Me" by the Uncle Kracker, which had been in first place before the terrorists struck. (AT&T Wireless customers can download songs of their choice onto their cellphones from the Internet at ringtoneslect. mobile.att.net.)

"The Star-Spangled Banner" got lots of competition on radio broadcasts. One popular song in the days after the attack was Ray Charles's version of "America the Beautiful." Lee Greenwood's "God Bless the U.S.A." and Kate Smith's "God Bless America," recorded in 1938, twenty years after it was written by Irvin Berlin, got some attention, but Americans seemed to want to hear "The Star-Spangled Banner" more. Those most favored were the versions by Whitney Houston, whose 1991 version from the Super Bowl during Gulf War days was rereleased as a single by Arista Records, and by Jimi Hendrix, in a recording made at Woodstock in 1969.

Sports events were called off for a week after the attack, and when they resumed, the television networks broadcast the playing of the anthem before the games instead of cutting away for commercials as they had done in the past. Whether that will continue remains to be seen. Some baseball teams marked the seventh-inning stretch by playing the unofficial anthem, "God Bless America," instead of "Take Me Out to the Ball Game." Whether that will continue, too, also remains to be seen, but baseball's connection with the Star-Spangled Banner—both the flag and the song—was reinforced on September 11, 2001, as the nation once again sang about the land of the free and the home of the brave.

Appendix

There are various versions of "The Star-Spangled Banner" with minor variations. They use contractions, like "o'er" in place of "over" in order to keep to the rhythm of the music. The following is the version provided by the State Department to American embassies abroad.

The Star-Spangled Banner

★   ★   ★

Oh, say, can you see, by the dawn's early light,
What so proudly we hail'd at the twilight's last gleaming?
Whose broad stripes and bright stars, thro' the perilous
fight,

O'er the ramparts we watch'd, were so gallantly streaming?
And the rockets' red glare, the bombs bursting in air,
Gave proof thro' the night that our flag was still there.
O say, does that star-spangled banner yet wave
O'er the land of the free and the home of the brave?

On the shore dimly seen thro' the mists of the deep,
Where the foe's haughty host in dread silence reposes,
What is that which the breeze, o'er the towering steep,
As it fitfully blows, half conceals, half discloses?
Now it catches the gleam of the morning's first beam,
In full glory reflected, now shines on the stream:
'T is the star-spangled banner: O, long may it wave
O'er the land of the free and the home of the brave!

And where is that band who so vauntingly swore
That the havoc of war and the battle's confusion
A home and a country should leave us no more?
Their blood has wash'd out their foul footsteps' pollution.
No refuge could save the hireling and slave
From the terror of flight or the gloom of the grave:
And the star-spangled banner in triumph doth wave
O'er the land of the free and the home of the brave.

O, thus be it ever when freemen shall stand,
Between their lov'd homes and the war's desolation;
Blest with vict'ry and peace, may the heav'n-rescued land
Praise the Pow'r that hath made and preserv'd us as a
nation!
Then conquer we must, when our cause it is just,

And this be our motto: "In God is our trust."
And the star-spangled banner in triumph shall wave
O'er the land of the free and the home of the brave!

★　　　★　　　★

A NATIONAL SYMBOL

Here is the text of a tribute to the American flag by Charles Evans Hughes, a former Chief Justice of the United States, provided by the National Flag Foundation:

The flag is the symbol of our national unity, our national endeavor, our national aspiration.

The flag tells of the struggle for independence, of union preserved, of liberty and union one and inseparable, of the sacrifices of brave men and women to whom the ideals and honor of this nation have been dearer than life.

It means America first; it means an undivided allegiance.

It means America united, strong and efficient, equal to her tasks.

It means that you cannot be saved by the valor and devotion of your ancestors, that to each generation comes its patriotic duty; and that upon your willingness to sacrifice and endure as those before you have sacrificed and endured rests the national hope.

It speaks of equal rights, of the inspiration of

free institutions exemplified and vindicated, of liberty under law intelligently conceived and impartially administrated. There is not a thread in it but scorns self-indulgence, weakness, and rapacity. It is eloquent of our community interests, outweighing all divergencies of opinion, and of our common destiny.

THE WORLD'S LARGEST FLAG

The world's largest flag, according to the *Guinness Book of World Records*, which ought to know about such things, is an American flag that is 505 by 225 feet and weighs 3,000 pounds. It was made by Humphrey's Flag Company of Pottstown, Pennsylvania, in 1992 for Thomas (Ski) Demski of Long Beach, California. It requires 500 people to unfurl it and was first displayed on Flag Day, June 14, 1993, at the Washington Monument. Demski also has a flag tatooed on his chest, according to *Guinness*. It is smaller.

HISTORIC SITES

When in Baltimore, you may wish to pay a visit to The Flag House. It is located at 844 East Pratt Street, and is open from 10 A.M. to 4 P.M. Tuesday through Saturday. For more information, call (410) 837-1793.

The Fort McHenry National Monument and Historic Shrine is a short drive from downtown Baltimore, just off I-95 at the end of East Fort Avenue. It is open from 8 A.M. to 5 P.M., but stays open later during the summer. The Fort is open every day except Christmas and New Year's Day. For more information, call (410) 962-4290, or visit the website at www.nps.gov/fomc.

Acknowledgments

This book had its beginnings in articles that I wrote for *The New York Times* on the conservation of the flag that inspired Francis Scott Key to write the poem that became our national anthem. I am grateful to The *Times* for giving me permission to pursue this book, as well as for providing a professional home for me for the past thirty-four years. Special thanks are due to Cornelia Dean, The *Times*'s science editor, who proposed an article on the conservation project and came up with such a sparkling display that it drew the attention of the book's publisher.

The book was suggested by Doug Grad, a senior editor at Dutton, for which I thank him as well as for his expert guidance.

My agent, Agnes Birnbaum, of Bleecker Street Associates, has been, as usual, superb.

Two employees at the Fort McHenry National Monument and Historic Shrine, Scott S. Sheads, a park ranger and historian, and Anna R. von Lunz, a museum curator, were extremely generous in showing me the fort where the Star-Spangled Banner flew and in answering my questions, helping me to find illustrations and reviewing parts of my manuscript. Scott has done an enormous amount of research into the fort and has written several books on it and the War of 1812. Anyone wanting to learn more about the subject of this book ought to turn first to Scott's books. In this day, when federal service is sometimes demeaned, I would propose that people look at the work of Anna, Scott and their colleagues in the National Park Service to see that we are getting good value for our taxes.

A great deal of research was performed for me in Britain, particularly on the heroic Major General Robert Ross, by John Mason, associate lecturer at the School of Social Science, Middlesex University.

Another source of information outside the United States, particularly on the American attack on Toronto, which is largely unknown in this country, was Dr. Carl Benn, chief curator of the City of Toronto Museum and Heritage Services. I thank him for reviewing sections of my manuscript.

Tables constructed by Professor Robert C. Sahr, a political scientist at Oregon State University, allowed me to express costs of things like the Star-Spangled Banner in today's dollars. He has calculated the comparative value of dollars back to 1800 and has provided advice to me for this book and for articles that I have written for *The New York Times*.

I thank several people at the Smithsonian Institution, including David Umansky, the institution's main spokesman; Melinda Machado, the spokeswoman of the Smithsonian's National Museum of American History, and two experts on the flag at that museum, Suzanne Thomassen-Krauss and Lonn Taylor.

I thank the experts and staff at the Library of Congress, particularly Craig D'Ooge, of the public affairs office.

It was a lot more difficult than I had imagined to work on this book without asking for a leave of absence. To make it work, my wife, Iris, had to relieve me of my responsibility of cooking for the second thirty years of our marriage. She had been the main cook for the first thirty. Just another reason to love her.

Bibliography

Catton, Bruce, and William B. Catton. *The Bold and Magnificent Dream: America's Founding Years, 1492–1815.* Garden City, N.Y.: Doubleday & Co., 1978.

Dudley, William S., editor, and Crawford, Michael J., associate editor. *The Naval War of 1812, A Documentary History, Vol. I, 1812.* Washington, D.C.: Naval Historical Center, Department of the Navy, 1985.

Hickey, Donald R. *The War of 1812: A Forgotten Conflict.* Urbana, Ill.: University of Illinois Press, 1989.

Kallen, Stuart A. *The Star-Spangled Banner.* Edina, Minn.: Abdo & Daughters, 1994.

Kroll, Steven. *The Story of the Star-Spangled Banner: By Dawn's Early Light.* New York: Scholastic Inc., 1994.

Light, Jonathan Fraser. *The Cultural Encyclopedia of Baseball.* Jefferson, N.C.: McFarland, 1997.

Marasco, David. *David Marasco's Negro Leagues Pages.* http://pubweb.nwu.edu/~dmarasco/1918.html.

Meyer, Sam. *Paradoxes of Fame: The Francis Scott Key Story.* Annapolis, Md.: Eastwind Publishing, 1995.

Morris, Roger. *Cockburn and the British Navy in Transition: Admiral Sir George Cockburn, 1772–1853.* Exeter, England: University of Exeter Press, 1997.

New York State Commission to Commemorate the War of 1812 and the Composition of the Star-Spangled Banner. *Final Report, March 1, 1970–March 1, 1971.* Albany, N.Y.

Roosevelt, Theodore. *The Naval War of 1812, or the History of the United States Navy During the Last War with Great Britain.* New York: G. P. Putnam's Sons, 1882.

Seale, William. *The President's House.* Washington, D.C.: White House Historical Association with the Cooperation of the National Geographic Society, 1986.

Seeden, Margaret. *Star-Spangled Banner: Our Nation and Its Flag.* Washington, D.C.: National Geographic Society, 1993.

Sheads, Scott. *Fort McHenry.* Baltimore: Nautical and Aviation Publishing Company of America, 1995.

Smith, Margaret Bayard. *The First Forty Years of Washington Society in the Family Letters of Margaret Bayard Smith,* edited by Gaillard Hunt. New York: F. Ungar Publishing Company, 1965.

Taylor, Lonn. *The Star-Spangled Banner: The Flag That Inspired the National Anthem.* New York: National Museum of American History, Smithsonian Institution, in association with Harry N. Abrams, 2000.

Wellington. *Supplementary Despatches, Correspondence and Memoranda of the Duke of Wellington, Vol. IX,* edited by his son the Duke of Wellington. London: John Murray, 1862.

Whitecraft, Melissa. *Francis Scott Key.* New York: Franklin Watts, 1994.

Index